ARTHUR MILLER
in conversation

Steve Centola

Northhouse & Northhouse / Dallas

Library of Congress Cataloguing in Publication Data

Centola, Steve, 1952-
    Arthur Miller in Conversation / Steve Centola.
    p. cm.
    Includes bibliographical references and index
    ISBN 0-935061-51-7
    1. Miller, Arthur, 1915- --Interviews. 2. Dramatists,
American--20th Century--Interviews. I. Miller, Arthur, 1915- II.
Title.
PS3525.I5156Z58 1993
812",52--dc20   92-37358

ISBN 0-935061-51-7

The first interview in this volume was published as "The Will to
Live': An Interview with Arthur Miller" in *Modern Drama*. The
second interview was published as "Just Looking for a Home': A
Conversation with Arthur Miller" in *American Drama*.

Contemporary Research Press
P.O. Box 7240
Dallas, Texas 75209

Printed in the United States of America

Contents

Introduction

Whenever people hear the titles *Death of a Salesman* (1949) and *The Crucible* (1953), their first impulse, more likely than not, is to identify the plays' creator as one of the literary giants of the twentieth century, for these extraordinary dramas are universally regarded as classics of the modern theater. But the dramatist who is praised for having created such masterpieces is not usually celebrated for having written such plays as *After the Fall* (1964), *The Archbishop's Ceiling* (1977), or *The Ride Down Mount Morgan* (1991). Of course, Arthur Miller is the author of all of these plays--and of much more--yet his fame in his own country seems to rest exclusively on accomplishments that came very early in his career.

Ironically, the same is not true abroad. While Miller's early plays are regularly performed on stages all over Europe, his later plays also see frequent productions in front of highly receptive audiences. Miller's popularity abroad is immense, so much so that he may very well be America's most renowned playwright in Europe. Hardly a night goes by that one of his plays is not seeing production on one of the stages of a major European city.

With his celebrity status surging overseas, one has to wonder why appreciation of Miller's later achievements has been so slow in coming in his native land. One obvious explanation comes to mind. Critics in America have never attempted to disguise their insistence that Miller's later plays be measured against his early successes. While it may strike most theatergoers as unreasonable for critics to expect Miller to continue to produce works that match the excellence of *Death of a Salesman*, that is precisely what has happened to him throughout his career. Each new play has been greeted by reviews expressing disappointment with Miller for continually failing to write another *Death of a Salesman*. What adds a bittersweet irony to this situation is the fact that, while his new plays suffer by the comparison, revivals of early plays like *Death of a Salesman* continue to enjoy commercial success, thereby keeping Miller in the public eye, and ensuring his lasting reputation with American audiences.

Indeed, the production history of Miller's plays in the New York area over the past decade or two reflects this critical ambivalence toward the playwright's work. *Death of a Salesman* fared extremely well in Broadway revivals in 1975 and 1984; likewise, both *A View from the Bridge* (1956), in 1983, and *All My Sons* (1947), in 1987, won respectable notices during their Broadway runs; and *The Crucible* made a decent showing as the premiere production for the National Actors Theater in 1991. During the same time period, however, *The Creation of the World and Other Business* was savagely ridiculed in 1972; *The Archbishop's Ceiling*, in 1977, and *Elegy for a Lady* and *Some Kind of Love Story*, in 1982, were treated so poorly during preliminary runs in Washington, D.C., and New Haven that they failed even to make it to Broadway; *The American Clock* was closed after just two weeks in 1980, causing its backers to lose thousands of dollars; *Clara* and *I Can't Remember Anything* were thoroughly dismissed by reviewers in 1987; and *The Ride Down Mount Morgan* saw its premiere production in London in 1991, after Miller decided to stage his new play out of the States, as a protest against the hostile and excessively commercial New York theater.[1]

No further proof needs to be provided to conclude that American critics find Miller's later drama inferior to his early plays. Yet, such a conclusion fails to account for the considerable variation in critical assessments of *The Price* from its original New York production in 1968 to its Broadway revivals in 1979, 1985, and 1992.[2] Initially dismissed as thematically irrelevant and stylistically anachronistic, *The Price* recently won kudos and was specifically praised for seeming even "more pertinent than it has ever been."[3] It was as if the critics decided that this particular play had somehow improved with age, making successful revivals possible where initial production failed. Or perhaps changes over time in political climates and theatrical tastes and trends had something to do with the rather fickle treatment *The Price* received at the hands of New York theater critics. Unfortunately, no such explanation can sufficiently account for the hapless production history of *After the Fall* in the States.

When *After the Fall* was first produced on Broadway in 1964, it provoked a blistering attack; Miller was widely denounced for including in his play thinly disguised episodes from his often stormy and very public marriage to Marilyn Monroe.[4] Undoubtedly, much of the hostility was the result of poor timing on Miller's part since the play appeared too soon after the death of Monroe. But even twenty years later, in response to a superb Off-Broadway production that considerably downplayed the connection between Monroe and the play's central female character, Maggie, the critics still refused to judge the play strictly on its own merits. Even while pretending to downplay the significance of autobiographical elements in the play, several critics denounced the scandalous personal associations that make the play, in their estimation, little more than "self-pitying psychodrama."[5]

Curiously enough, though, a 1990 production of the play in London was not cursed with the same fate. Attempting once and for all to destroy any suggestion that Maggie need be played as Monroe, Michael Blakemore took a bold creative move by casting Josette Simon, a black actress, in the lead female role--a role which, incidentally, won the actress the British equivalent of a Tony award for her performance. Blakemore explained the play's success by simply noting that, in London, *After the Fall* was not "so mired in celebrity speculation that the meaning of the play was simply overlooked."[6]

While that may very well be the case, Christopher Bigsby offers another explanation of the reasons for the contrasting receptions to *After the Fall* in Europe and America. According to Bigsby, Europeans react more favorably to Miller's later plays because they share with the playwright a belief in "the cause-and-effect time connection implied in the '*After*' of '*After the Fall*.'"[7] "America does not want to be told that it lives after the fall," says Bigsby. In America, lost "innocence is recoverable."[8] Miller's tragic vision is more compatible with the perspective of Europeans who accept human imperfection and recognize the need to offset it with responsible social action. In his homeland, Bigsby contends, Miller's tragic vision of the human condition "collides with the American dream of strictly individual attainment."[9]

There is much to be said in support of Bigsby's persuasive assessment. The fervent belief in near infinite possibilities is almost an innate part of the American psyche. It is a cultural inheritance, so to speak; this integral part of the American dream "comes with the territory." But what Bigsby fails to realize is that Miller's tragic vision is distinctly American because it always allows for that single possibility inherent within the often nearly overwhelming givens and insurmountable odds against individual fulfillment. Miller does, indeed, refuse to suggest that anyone can recover lost innocence. But he gives his audiences much more hope than that which is created through lies and self-delusion. His plays offer real hope, the kind of hope he so impressively depicts in *After the Fall*; hope that can be reclaimed if the individual, recognizing his imperfections and capacity to commit the most horrible atrocities, accepts the freedom to choose and takes responsibility for all willfully chosen actions. Even in the most absurd of situations--as Miller so powerfully shows us in both *Incident At Vichy* (1964) and *Playing for Time* (1980), an individual has the freedom to resist oppression and forge new values in the face of the most terrible adversity. And such hope is always a part of his tragic vision--from *The Man Who Had All The Luck* (1944) to *The Ride Down Mount Morgan*. No matter how slim the chances, the possibility for personal salvation is always there. Whether an individual has the courage and strength to face adversity and the truth about oneself ultimately determines whether the person triumphs or despairingly accepts defeat.

Over the years, Miller has shown his audience both responses to the tragic circumstances befalling his characters. Occasionally, particularly in his later plays, his characters peer into the dark recesses of their souls and find there a glimmer of hope for human redemption. Quentin, in *After the Fall*, Von Berg, in *Incident at Vichy*, and Fania Fenelon, in *Playing for Time*, learn that living with the knowledge of one's complicity in evil can be almost more unbearable, and tragic, than death itself. But without such knowledge, suggests Miller, there can be no hope for humanity. Often, especially in his early drama, his characters lack the necessary strength to rise above despair. Joe Keller in *All My Sons*, Willy Loman in *Death of a Salesman*, Eddie Carbone in *A View from the Bridge*, and Maggie in *After the Fall*--all succumb to a terrible drive toward self-destruction that comes from living in bad faith and attempting to escape from responsibility for the life created by their actions. Their desperation drives them to suicide, but all the while Miller shows other possibilities existed if only they had the courage to accept their personal culpability.

The will to live--a recurrent theme in Miller's canon--was mentioned by Miller in our first discussion. In response to my observation that his drama conveys an optimistic toughness, Miller insisted that, in spite of what critics often write about his work, he is not a pessimist. He expressed a childlike reverence for nature and said he was constantly fascinated by the lesson of life, the struggle toward survival that is everywhere around us. There is too much evidence of the will to live to abandon hope. His assertions clearly revealed strong convictions and suggested that not only had Miller imbued his plays with this potent spirit, but he probably also drew from such convictions the kind of strength he has periodically needed to bounce back from the artistic setbacks that have plagued him throughout his career.

Our first meeting occurred not long after *The American Clock* (1980) saw its dismal Broadway production cut short. Little did Miller know at the time, but his two new one-act plays, *Elegy for a Lady* and *Some Kind of Love Story* (1982), were about to meet a similar fate in New Haven. Coincidentally, at the time, Miller was also preparing for his trip to China, in 1983, where he would be directing *Death of a Salesman*. He seemed amused by the critics who insisted that the play would never work in a communist country. As Miller was to write later, in his memoirs about his experiences directing the play in Chinese, he knew all along that he could reach the Chinese people because at bottom, "there is one humanity"[10] Once again, Miller would prove his critics wrong. As had happened repeatedly in the States and all over the western world, *Death of a Salesman* was a tremendous success and elicited standing ovations from the audiences--a rare gesture of appreciation from the Chinese. The quintessentially American play spoke to the Chinese and touched "the heart's common ground."[11]

Miller's success in China was matched by a series of highly successful productions of his plays in Europe--particularly in Great Britain--during the following decade. In 1986, revised versions of *The American Clock* and *The Archbishop's Ceiling* played to enthusiastic audiences in London; in 1987, *The Golden Years*, a previously unpublished apprentice play, was performed on radio by the BBC; in 1990, at least five of his plays were produced on the London stage, including splendid productions of *After the Fall* and the rarely performed *The Man Who Had All the Luck*; in 1991, *The Ride Down Mount Morgan* received its world premiere in London; and in 1992, while *All My Sons* and *The Crucible* played to responsive audiences in London, Miller directed *Death of a Salesman* in Stockholm.[12]

Of course, the kind of incredible success he has enjoyed abroad makes Miller's problems at home even that much more noticeable. As Matt Wolf accurately points out, "Almost play by play, one can contrast a failed New York production with its successful British counterpart. . . ."[13] The production history of *The American Clock* in the States and in Great Britain provides a striking example of what has become a familiar contrast. When it first appeared on Broadway in 1980, *The American Clock* was panned by virtually every critic and was canceled just two weeks into the production. In 1986, however, it ran the entire season at the National Theatre and received an Olivier Award nomination for best play on the British stage that year.[14]

Undeniably, the huge success of this play in London can at least partially be attributed to the fact that Miller had extensively revised the play before it had its London production. Yet, ironically, his revisions were designed to return the play to its original form. Commenting on his play's failure to find an audience in the States, Miller blames himself for allowing external pressures to cause him to make artistic compromises that weakened his drama. He specifically admits to having reworked *The American Clock* before its original New York production to appease his critics: "as with *The Archbishop's Ceiling*, I had hopelessly given way and reshaped a play for what I had come to think of as the Frightened Theatre."[15] Through subsequent revisions, however, he rectified the problems with his text and in 1986, both *The American Clock* and *The Archbishop's Ceiling* were performed in England "in their early, uncontaminated versions."[16]

It has been over six years since these plays enjoyed successful productions abroad, yet the "uncontaminated" and critically acclaimed versions have yet to see Broadway productions. Again, one has to ask why is Miller's later work shunned in the States. Given his continued interest in exploring tragic situations, a possible explanation for the treatment may be that his subject matter is too disturbing for the "entertainment district." After all, the number of serious plays on the Broadway stage at any given time is extraordinarily small. Perhaps the high cost of production has something to do with the problem, and producers interested only in profits are unwilling to take necessary risks on plays like Miller's. Or perhaps the exorbitant ticket price causes New York audiences to go the theater wanting only to escape, not to reflect on human tragedy or to have their values challenged.

Commenting on his recent setbacks in the American theater, Miller writes: "I had not had the luck to fall in with people sufficiently at ease with psychopolitical themes to set them in a theatrical style, a challenge more often tackled in the British theatre."[17] Gone is the bold and direct confrontation with one's destiny. Americans, instead, says Miller, "had come to prize and celebrate in our art disconnection for its own sake, but this was not at all the same as tearing apart the givens of experience in order to recreate a fresh unity that would inform us about our lives."[18] And that, of course, is precisely what Miller strives to achieve in all of his drama--a unity that derives from the force of his inspired insight into the individual psyche and the shared human condition. His is a drama that asks ultimate questions and challenges assumptions by forcing its audiences to face the tragic implications of conscious existence. Miller's dramatic action is usually riveting; his thematic content is always provocative. His is not a drama for the faint-hearted, for Miller's plays are never escapist.

Miller has been as fearless in tackling hard issues and in facing adversity in his private life as he has been in his artistic one. His heroic stand before the House Committee on Un-American Activities in 1956 is now legendary. Echoing the courageous words and noble sentiments that his John Proctor, facing the Salem Witchcraft Trials, expressed on the Broadway stage three years before Miller's testimony, Miller refused to turn informant against friends and acquaintances. His insistence that he would not bring harm upon another person sent shock waves through Congress. In his role as President of International PEN, Miller similarly offended government leaders from China to Chile by actively campaigning for the release of imprisoned artists. His protest of the Vietnam War did much to alienate him from his own government's administration at the time, just as his open and frequent criticism of the commercial New York theater and its critics has done much to strain his relations with both the media and the arbiters of the entertainment culture in his own homeland.

In my second talk with Miller, perhaps even more so than in our first conversation, Miller's disillusionment with the American government was evident. Miller often illustrated his points about thematic interests in his plays by punctuating his discussion of his art with anecdotes about current political affairs. For example, in discussing another important recurring motif in his drama, particularly in the later plays--that is, the power of illusion--Miller cited stories linking the CIA to drug smuggling in Indonesia to illustrate how easily one can begin to form doubts about the nature of the real. In his voice, I could hear his genuine disillusionment with the country that has turned the American dream into a nightmare, but there was also the sense that the surface issues functioned mostly as convenient metaphors to exemplify a universal dilemma confronting humanity.

Clearly, Miller, the private man, feels as strongly as Miller, the playwright, about the problems posing the biggest threat to humanity's survival. Pollution, drug dependence, teenage suicide-- these had now become the serious threats that were symptomatic of a graver illness, a deeper problem affecting the nation. And, while the issues may have changed over the years, it was still clear that Miller remains committed to analyzing and rectifying the ills of American society.

In both interviews, as in both phases of his career, Miller had much to say about responsibility. While acknowledging that tremendous pressure is exerted upon the individual by society and other deterministic forces, Miller still believes that individuals, within certain limitations, have the freedom to choose their destinies. Certainly, the ability to choose is evident throughout Miller's drama: from Proctor's denunciation of the Salem Court in *The Crucible,* through Von Berg's defiance of the Nazis in *Incident at Vichy,* and on to Kroll's tragic affirmation of the need for the liberal values that indirectly cause his daughter's murder in *Clara*. But Miller always shows that such freedom also has its cost: sometimes it necessitates the loss of one's own life, as in *The Crucible* and *Incident at Vichy*; or even worse, sometimes, it requires the acceptance of the death of a loved one, as in *Clara*. One thing is certain: in Miller's drama, freedom also means responsibility. And the obligation that such a burden carries may ultimately be the single most important factor in preventing humanity from destroying itself.

The potential for mass destruction that always threatens humanity is most powerfully conveyed in *After the Fall* with a striking scenic image: the shadows of concentration camp towers looming across the stage. The Biblical allusion contained within the title of this play suggests much about the central underlying and unifying theme in Miller's plays. In his foreword to *After the Fall*, Miller indicates that the conflicts he explores as a play-wright, and the dilemmas he sees confronting humanity, have their origin in the Bible with the choices contained within Eden:

> And two alternatives open out of Eden. One is Cain's alternative--or if you will Oswald's; to express without limit one's unbridled inner compulsion, in this case to murder and to plead unawareness as a virtue and a defense. The other course is what roars through the rest of the Bible and all history--the struggle of the human race through the millennia to pacify the destructive impulses of man, to express his wishes for greatness, for wealth, for accomplishment, for love, but without turning law and peace into chaos.

Miller's hope in the individual's ability to make the right choice has not diminished even though his plays sometimes fail to give that impression. Perhaps Miller simply feels compelled to create drama that always keeps before its audiences the rather poignant reminder that, as he indicated at our last interview, "there is far more that we could do to make a home of the world than we are doing--by acting responsibly. . . ." It is a message that reverberates throughout his canon--as well as throughout the two interviews that follow.

Notes

[1] For additional information on the production history of Miller's plays, see the following: Christopher Bigsby, *Arthur Miller and Company* (London: Methuen, 1990); Bigsby, *File on Miller* (London: Methuen, 1988); Arthur Miller, *Timebends* (New York: Grove Press, 1987); and Matt Wolf, "An Exile of Sorts Finds a Welcome." *New York Times*, 13 October 1991, Sec. H, p. 6.

[2] Contrast, for example, the following two reviews: Robert Brustein, "The Unseriousness of Arthur Miller." *New Republic* 24 February 1968: 39-41, and David Richards, "'The Price' Is Right for These Days." *New York Times*, 28 June 1992, Sec. H, pp. 5, 14.

[3] Richards, p. H5.

[4] See Brustein, "Arthur Miller's Mea Culpa." *New Republic* 8 February 1964: 26-28, 30.

[5] Richard Corliss, "Wounds That Will Not Heal." *Time* 15 October 1984: 113. Also see: Edith Oliver, "The Theatre." *New Yorker* 15 October 1984: 158, and Frank Rich, "Theater: '*After the Fall*' Is Revived." *New York Times*, 5 October 1984, Sec. C, p. 3.

[6] Michael Blakemore, Quoted in *Arthur Miller and Company*, p. 142.

[7] Bigsby, Quoted by John Drybred, "Scholarly Conference Closes Arthur Miller Festival at MU." *Lancaster Intelligencer Journal*, 11 April 1992, Sec. B, p. 1.

[8] Bigsby, Quoted by Drybred, p. B1.

[9] Bigsby, Quoted by Drybred, p. B2.

[10] Miller, *"Salesman" in Beijing* (New York: Viking, 1984), p. 11.

[11] Miller, *"Salesman" in Beijing*, p. 249.

[12]For more information on Miller's successes abroad, see Bigsby, *Arthur Miller and Company*; Bigsby, *File on Miller*; Miller, *Timebends*; and Wolf, p. H6.

[13]Wolf, p. H6.

[14]Wolf, p. H6.

[15]Miller, *Timebends*, p. 586.

[16]Miller, *Timebends*, p. 587.

[17]Miller, *Timebends*, p. 586.

[18]Miller, *Timebends*, p. 587.

[19]Miller, "Foreword to *After the Fall*." In *The Theater Essays of Arthur Miller*, Ed. Robert A. Martin (New York: Penguin, 1978), pp. 255-256.

June 25, 1982

S.R.C. I've always been fascinated by your ability to maintain a singleness of vision in plays remarkably different from each other in form, style, mood, theme, characterization, plot, and even at times in language. Would you agree that this underlying continuity in your work derives from a vision of the human condition that can be described as a kind of existential humanism--a vision that emphasizes self-determinism and social responsibility and that is optimistic and affirms life by acknowledging man's possibilities in the face of his limitations and even sometimes in the dramatization of his failures?

ARTHUR MILLER That's very good. I would agree with that. That's a fair summary of what I feel about it--my own views about it.

S.R.C. The one play that seems to provide the clearest revelation of your vision is *After the Fall*.

ARTHUR MILLER Just about, yes.

S.R.C. Not many people see it that way.

ARTHUR MILLER Well, I think they were, to be quite frank--I've said this before; it's no news--but I think that they were blinded by the gossip and the easy way out. But it's not just in my work. I think people go for tags for any writer; you don't have to think about what he's doing any longer, especially if he's around a long time. But then simply you know what you think you want to expect. It may or may not have much to do with what he's doing. But, they find whatever in the work fits that expectation, and the other is simply not dealt with or is rejected. This is an old story here that we all know.

S.R.C. Your vision, what I've called your existential humanism, seems to have a lot in common with Jean-Paul Sartre's existentialist philosophy.

ARTHUR MILLER You know that Sartre did the screenplay for *The Crucible*, and we were on the verge of meeting three or four times and never managed to because he was out of France when I was there. There was always a mix-up, and I always thought that there was more time than there actually turned out to be. But I think there was a relationship which was not programmatic in any way. It just means people leaning in the same kind of direction.

S.R.C. So you wouldn't say it was a matter of influence?

ARTHUR MILLER No, no.

S.R.C. Would you feel as though I were going for a tag if I pointed out some of the similarities between your vision and Sartre's existentialism?

ARTHUR MILLER Well, I don't think that's a danger because he certainly was always attractive to me in a vague way. But I'll tell you, I'm not a methodical, philosophical writer; I don't spring out of that kind of tradition. I work out of instinct. And so whatever similarities that there turn out to be, somebody's always related to something.

S.R.C. Do you think an identification of these Sartrean correspondences in your plays could bring out the metaphysical issues in your work and help to put to rest the notion that you're merely a social realist, the tag which you seem to have been stuck with for some time now?

ARTHUR MILLER The social realist thing is what they were doing with Ibsen all his life. He was supposed to be interested in sewers because of *An Enemy of the People*, or in syphilis because of *Ghosts*, or in women's rights or something like that because of *A Doll's House*, and all the rest of it. Of course, what is inevitable is that these are all, in a certain sense, metaphors, and had the writer merely been interested in sewers, violence, women's rights, and the rest of it, we would have long since lost track of his name. These are metaphorical situations of the human race as it goes on forever.

S.R.C. The great writer gets at the universal through the particular.

ARTHUR MILLER Sure. If you don't, you end up with a kind of blatantly philosophical dialogue of some sort that nobody really is interested in. It isn't the way these obtrude into experience. That's as simple as it can be.

S.R.C. I read some of your unpublished works that I was able to get through the Humanities Research Center at the University of Texas. One of these was a letter you wrote called "Willy and the Helpless Giant," and in that letter you suggest that tragedy results when one tries to attain honor by putting on a mask and performing for the public instead of being what one really is and does best. In many ways, that idea parallels Sartre's distinction between being-for-itself and being-for-others. I'm wondering if that conflict isn't part of the tragedy of modern existence: individuals feel obligated to adopt poses or wear masks in order to make themselves feel significant or honorable?

ARTHUR MILLER That's true. But the question is how old a procedure that is, how old that process is. Because the more class-structured a society is (for example, a royal society like, let's say, the eighteenth-century or seventeenth-century French society), people had to fit into a mold that was given them by the class that they felt they belonged to. And all costume, dress, manners, habits, and the mores were predetermined, in effect, so that sincerity was hardly a value at all. It's just that it wasn't necessarily cynical. It was simply that the society and sincerity could not comfortably coexist. So that for the sake of good order, one had to adopt some kind of persona, which is not necessarily the one that one really has. Now, for us, I think this is an old thing in the United States. Alexis de Tocqueville mentions the fact that we don't want to be set apart from the mob. That means people will adopt a mask in order to be like everybody else. And maybe it's implicit in that statement that Americans don't want to be separated from the mask.

S.R.C. That's an interesting way of establishing a connection with others.

ARTHUR MILLER But there's also a price to pay for that. And the price, obviously, is the loss of something. Society makes such a heavy demand upon the individual that he has to give up his individuality (and we do have a high percentage of mental breakdowns and neuroses and the rest of it). So, maybe it goes along with democracy, oddly enough.

S.R.C. That's interesting.

ARTHUR MILLER I think that the British, for example, are far more able and willing to endure characters than we are. (What would you call characters? People who don't necessarily abide by the rules.) We're much less tolerant. We won't lend them money; we won't see them through school sometimes. We impose a discipline on them because they are different, and so on.

S.R.C. So we place a greater emphasis on conformity?

ARTHUR MILLER Conformity is a terrific power here. To jump to another sector of this, I think it lay behind the power of the Un-American Activities Committee, because, after all, what they were threatening most people with was not jail; and it certainly wasn't shooting; it was being disgraced--social disgrace.

S.R.C. What I was getting at in that question is whether tragedy could be considered as a fundamental condition of being. Take Hamlet as an example. Here's an individual who is obsessed with living up to the image expected of him by others. It's the same with Othello and Oedipus. It seems that all these characters find themselves torn between. . . .

ARTHUR MILLER Mask and reality. You ought to look into the whole question of the fact that the Greek plays were played in masks. I'm not sure where that fits here, but it just occurred to me. Well, of course, I have been very conscious of this as a writer, that is, of the conflict, the friction, the opposition between the individual and his social obligations, his social mask, his social self. And it always seemed to me that the perfect society would be one in which that gap, that friction, would be able to be minimized, but people don't seem to be driven crazy about it. It isn't that totally American kind of a thing, though, obviously. It's everywhere; it just takes different shapes. I suspect it's in tribal Africa. You see, there are social duties and social fears that can create a tragic event.

S.R.C. That's why I mentioned Sartre; he's dealing with the fundamental condition of being human: being self-conscious.

ARTHUR MILLER It's certainly in the center of it.

S.R.C. Well, it seems that the tragedy of displacement, which you have discussed in your essays, is really a type of existential crisis that results when one has to make a conscious choice between his public self and his private one. You say that displacement results from a character's violation of his nature through compromises or mistakes. And then his effort to regain his sense of identity against overwhelming obstacles makes the play take on a tragic dimension.

ARTHUR MILLER I think in the plays of mine that I felt were of tragic dimensions, the characters are obsessed with retrieving a lost identity, meaning that they were displaced by the social pressure, the social mask, and no longer could find themselves, or are on the verge of not being able to. There in the private man is the real one.

S.R.C. In your Introduction to your *Collected Plays*, Volume I, you say that the one unseen goal toward which almost all of your plays strive is the "discovery and its proof--that we are made and yet are more than what made us." That statement seems to pinpoint the central tension underlying all of your plays, a tension created by the antagonistic forces of fate and free will acting upon each other.

ARTHUR MILLER Right, Did you ever read my first play on Broadway which failed, called *The Man Who Had All the Luck*? In the line of this kind of discussion, that really was a very important play for me, because while the play failed, I learned in that play where I was positioned in the world, so to speak. And the play taught me something which I wasn't even aware of at the moment. But looking back--just this kind of a question is raised. He wants to know where he begins and the world begins; where he leaves off, the world begins. He's trying really to separate himself and to control his destiny.

S.R.C. Or to make himself aware that he has been controlling it, and that he's not just a pawn of the forces around him.

ARTHUR MILLER Yes, right. So, it goes right back to the beginning in the most vague part of my career.

S.R.C. That play didn't get the justice it deserved because the critics misunderstood it. If I'm not mistaken, a major complaint at the time was that the play displayed "jumbled philosophies" because you didn't choose to advocate either fate or free will. But why should you choose one and not see the interplay?

ARTHUR MILLER The interplay was the point! Well, you see, this was where they couldn't run with a tag. That's exactly what I started out by saying today. Had I been very clever and sophisticated about it, I would have thrown out a tag that they could run with and feel that they had it in their pocket. But I let the tension run on right through the end, instead of resolving it for them the way it never is in life.

S.R.C. So you would say that dialectic exists also in your other plays?

ARTHUR MILLER Oh, yeah. No question about it. It goes right on now.

S.R.C. Like Sartre, you often seem to concern yourself with the alienation of the individual in your plays. Frequently, alienation has something to do with the individual's recognition of (and reluctance to accept) his separateness. Such alienation is perhaps most apparent in *After the Fall*, but it is also evident in your other plays. Willy Loman and other characters also cannot accept the fact that they are separate beings.

ARTHUR MILLER That's right. You know, I have a line somewhere--oh, I think it's in an Introduction I wrote to *A View from the Bridge* or one of the editions of *A View from the Bridge*, but I could be wrong about this because it's now twenty years or more--to the effect that the underlying tension is that man is looking for a home. In other words, he's looking for an unalienated existence, and this can be terribly attractive and seductive and is the root of a lot of mystery. See, one of the greatest appeals of Christianity as well as of Communism is that it promises to end alienation. If I want to subjugate man, I can declare alienation a sin, and anybody who is alienated or causes anyone else to be alienated should be punished. See, this is what the Puritans did among themselves. This is what the Communist party does in Russia. And this is what the loyal extreme patriots in every country do. They're always against aliens, just as simple as that. It's the root of anti-foreignism; it's the root of this philistinism that we're always confronting. And everybody does it! The function of a group is to define itself, and its definition is: "We are us, and you are you." You see?

S.R.C. Isn't that a type of psychological projection? Couldn't people who create these groups of others, or outsiders, just as easily say: "We are good, and you are evil?"

ARTHUR MILLER Absolutely. "We are us."

S.R.C. And they project everything they don't like about themselves onto others?

ARTHUR MILLER Absolutely. That's what it's all about. It's a form of psychological warfare. My view from the beginning has more or less been (it has shifted with each play to a certain degree) to find a form, in effect, for the condition of tension, rather than resolution of this particular dichotomy through consciousness, through being aware that indeed I am alienated. I'm not you, but that doesn't mean because I'm not you that I can't sympathize with you. Well, to maintain that kind of tension in all of the thing, especially in political and social existence, we're without and refuse to resolve it. You might be able to, but the solution is always false. That's the difficulty. And in a play, it's very aggravating for the audience.

S.R.C. Not for the dramatist?

ARTHUR MILLER No. It's a condition of existence. In fact, you could almost say that the tragic view is that it is tragic because of the fact that it's unresolvable. We wish so for a pillow to lay our head upon, and it's a stone.

S.R.C. So man is always alienated, and yet he is constantly striving to get beyond his condition.

ARTHUR MILLER Right.

S.R.C. There's something dignified in his effort though.

ARTHUR MILLER I was just about to say that the whole point of it is that the aspiration is holy. See, the Biblical prophets are terrific because they refused to compromise. They maintained the tension through people like Ezekiel or Isaiah. Isaiah will project the plowshares and the peacemakers will be blessed and all the rest of it, but that's the aspiration. The implicit fact is that they're not around yet, these blessed people.

S.R.C. So what makes the characters tragic is partially the fact that only a few people, perhaps, ever attain that kind of self-recognition, or get to the point where they try to transcend their condition?

ARTHUR MILLER Right.

S.R.C. So the great mass of people aren't moved this way, or at least aren't aware of it?

ARTHUR MILLER The great mass of people are in the chorus. They perceive perfectly well what's happening, or very often. But, for whatever reason, they are bereft of the power or the lust for the power or the sacrificial nature that is required to go seeking. You know, the other day with that case, the Hinckley case, is a very good example of something like this. Now this was a jury, I think, of almost all black people, and they gave this perfectly horrible (to most people) verdict. And then people said, "Well, that's because they're so dumb, you know; they aren't educated people." Well, they interviewed them on television, and they were remarkably sophisticated. And they dug it very, very well. They were really on a knife-edge, and they reacted in a very sharp and profound way: they blamed the code. And they said: "That's the code, and that is all the choice we had by that code." Well, that's terrific. See, now there's an instance of people who perforce were put in a position of having to make moral decisions, which normally in ordinary life they wouldn't be required to do, not in a public way certainly. My point is that you don't have to be a "noble" creature. This is changing the subject slightly, but since you raised the question of most people, this is certainly most people. These were blacks in Washington, D.C. They dug it; they understood it perfectly.

S.R.C. So, it's just that most people usually aren't placed in that position, or they prefer not to be?

ARTHUR MILLER Or they prefer not to be!

S.R.C. But everyone could experience this same fate, this same tragic existence?

ARTHUR MILLER Sure. Absolutely everyone as far as social rank is concerned.

S.R.C. In an interview a few years ago, you said that Americans seem to have a "primordial fear of falling." I was wondering if you thought Americans, more that anyone else, have that feeling because it goes with the territory?

ARTHUR MILLER   I think that that is more American than any other country, yeah, in my observation. I think that we are more afraid of losing caste, losing our hard-won place in the middle class. People will kill for that. I think that that causes more racial hatred and hostility and fear than anything else. Incidentally, I regard racism as a class phenomenon. I was born in Harlem, and I saw it happen in Harlem--I think I did, anyway. That's been my reason for it: that blacks are not acceptable more for the fact that they are working-class or poor than because they are black. If in a short period of time by some miracle there were hundreds and hundreds of thousands of black professionals, middle-class people, the thing would begin to fade. We're seeing it now with the Arabs, the sheiks, the wealthy Arab who was formerly a creature of ridicule. Well, now he can come in and buy up a whole city. With a new class identity he starts to take on a new kind of persona, a new kind of dignity. It isn't so jokey any more to see somebody walking around in those funny clothes which might conceal millions.

S.R.C. So most people chase their American dreams because they know that success determines how much they are accepted by others.

ARTHUR MILLER   No question about it.

S.R.C. In *Incident at Vichy*, Leduc tells the others as they await examination that they have been trained to die, to be willing victims for their persecutors. I'm wondering if he implies in that statement that death is often preferable to life for those who would have to live without illusions. And, once again, isn't such self-deception a peculiarly American trait?   Haven't we been trained to see the world through rose-tinted glasses?   Aren't we essentially a nation of people incapable of coping with reality?

ARTHUR MILLER Yes. I think that tremendous power does that to people, incidentally. The British did it for two centuries as their power got tremendous. They were able to enforce their wishes upon the world. So they wished more than they observed. I think they were primarily that way, and I think the Germans were able to do this once where they had the power to do it. It goes with power; it goes with the territory.

S.R.C. I'm going to take a different direction here. Some critics have complained about Charley's speech in the Requiem in *Death of a Salesman*, saying that it's out of character for a realist like Charley to be making sentimental speeches about dreams.

ARTHUR MILLER It's not even sentimental. You know that speech is almost a handbook of what you've got to think if you're going to be a salesman. Under the circumstances, of course, it is said over a grave, so naturally it is full of feeling and mourning. But it is objective information, so to speak; it is absolutely real. Those are the visionary qualities that make salesmen tick.

S.R.C. Aren't you also doing in this play what Fitzgerald does with Nick in his portrayal of Gatsby? In other words, you have a character who is fairly objective throughout the work make that statement over the grave because it can carry more weight coming from him, a realist.

ARTHUR MILLER You're right! That speech is the obverse of the early speech that Charley makes in the play to Willy when he says: "Why must everybody like you? Who liked J.P. Morgan?" Which is an absolutely dead-on, existentialist kind of way of looking at salesmanship. This is the obverse of it. He knows damn well what Willy was feeling; that's why he can make that speech to him. This is now said as the obverse of the other, but it's complementary. These are two halves of the same thing.

S.R.C. In an interview with Ronald Hayman some years ago, you defined fate as "high probability" and said that it is what happens "when a man starts out to do what he intends to do . . . [and] creates forces which he never bargained for, but whose contradictions nevertheless spring directly from the force of his thrust." Would you say that this is the kind of fate that's in the background of plays like *All My Sons, Death of a Salesman*, and *The Price?*

ARTHUR MILLER Yes.

S.R.C. Many of the characters in these plays seem to believe that they have no free will. But don't they have free will and just fail to consider all the consequences when they commit themselves to certain courses of action?

ARTHUR MILLER Right. And I would add that it's all but impossible to take into consideration most of the time.

S.R.C. We can't be that farsighted?

ARTHUR MILLER No, because the possibilities are too complex, too complicated, too infinite.

S.R.C. But, eventually, we have to accept what we do; we can't say we are excused from responsibility because the consequence was beyond our realm of control.

ARTHUR MILLER Right. You started it. For me, the typical case of our time is the Oppenheimer thing. I use him as the symbol of the scientists who put together this ferocious world-ending trick hat. And what they were exercising was technical curiosity, a time-honored civilizing trait of mankind. And then it goes off, and as Oppenheimer says, he starts to quote Hindu scripture: "I've taken the shape of death. I started the dance and I end it by killing everyone."

S.R.C. I'm going to shift directions again. In *The Price*, Solomon says he would not know what to say to his daughter if she were to return from the grave. Isn't Solomon essentially saying that no one can transcend the bounds of human subjectivity?

ARTHUR MILLER That's a good way to put it.

S.R.C. Doesn't he imply that because each individual is totally and irremediably separated from the other, only each individual can take responsibility for what he is in life?

ARTHUR MILLER That's a very good way to put it. Yes. He accepts something there, doesn't he? He says, in effect: "I was the way I am; she is the way she was; and what happened was the inevitable result of that. So what could have changed it?"

S.R.C. "And if she comes back, I still can't change it. So just accept it as it is."

ARTHUR MILLER Right. There's a kind of a cosmic acceptance of the situation.

S.R.C. That kind of acceptance seems to occur in your plays where characters like Quentin, Leduc, Von Berg, or Solomon decide that they must accept what is and not try to mold reality to fit their perceptions of it.

ARTHUR MILLER Exactly. And from that comes not passivity but strength.

S.R.C. That sounds again very much like Sartre. Like you, he was also accused of being a pessimist, and he responded to the charge by saying: "I'm not a pessimist; I merely believe in optimistic toughness." Isn't that also what you're saying?

ARTHUR MILLER Right.

S.R.C. In *After the Fall,* both Rose and Elsie seem to betray the men they love because they want to deny their complicity in their husbands' problems in order to maintain their own innocence, a counterfeit innocence that helps them see themselves as victims.

ARTHUR MILLER Those particular women feel that they did not participate in the decision making (if you want to objectify the whole thing), so they are not going to submit to the victim- ization. And that separation takes place, in effect saying: "You made your bed, now lie in it; I'm not going to get in there with you." It's a reassertion of separateness, incidentally.

S.R.C. With that kind of separateness, though, isn't there also some kind of betrayal?

ARTHUR MILLER Sure. It's inevitable because the implicit, although largely unannounced, larceny behind their relationship is that they were irrevocably joined. Right? And it turns out, they're not. It turns out that when the interests change, the arrangement has to change. This isn't cynicism, though, to me. It's just the way it is.

S.R.C. I see Maggie in the play as a perfect illustration of the individual who counterfeits her innocence to appear as the helpless victim of others. I know you have spoken about this in some of your essays.

ARTHUR MILLER Yeah, right.

S.R.C. Would you say that Maggie is guilty of bad faith, of lying to herself or of trying to see only the illusions, more or less?

ARTHUR MILLER Sure. In a way she's dying of the lie, as Quentin says to her. It's the only time in the play that he's absolutely right. She's a slave to the idea of being victimized.

Oddly enough, it's a paradox that the awareness of being enslaved becomes the principle of the person. Instead of a key to freedom, it's a lock on the door. I guess it all comes down to a pact of nonrecognition with all human nature, which is what enslaves us all. And all these philosophical attempts are really, in one way or another, attempts toward a confrontation with the dialectic of how we operate.

S.R.C. So what she does is self-destructive because she makes herself be what she really doesn't want to be?

ARTHUR MILLER It's conformity to a perverse image. In one way or another, we're all involved with that, but for some people it's terminal.

S.R.C. In *After the Fall*, you seem to suggest that the original Fall, the Biblical Fall, is perpetually reenacted with each individual's fall into consciousness, his conflict with others, his struggle with his egotism, and his fundamental choice between good and evil, or as you have called it, his choice between Cain's and Abel's alternatives. Do you think that with the fall into consciousness comes the dilemma of choosing to live either for oneself or for others?

ARTHUR MILLER Well, people are threatened with freedom; it's the reaction to the threat of freedom. The fall is the fall from the arms of God, the right to live, to eat, to be conscious that there exists all the world. It's the fall from nonconscious existence and from the pleasant and unconscious slavery of childhood and so on. The fall is the threat of freedom, of having to make choices, instead of having them made for you.

S.R.C. In a few different places, you say that man is in the society and society is in the man, just as the fish is in the water and the water is in the fish. That statement reminds me of Jung, and I was wondering if you believe his theory about the individual carrying around with him in the collective unconscious, deep within his psyche, the cargo of his ancestral past.

ARTHUR MILLER Yeah. I've often been tempted to believe that, although, of course, it's unprovable. And in my own case, I think, for example, I was never really a religious person in any conventional sense. I didn't even make sense out of the Bible until fairly recent years, if you can make sense out of the Bible. Yet, all of the ideas that we are talking about now are stemming from the Old Testament. The more I live, the more I think that somewhere down the line it poured into my ear, and I don't even know when or how. But I'm reading it again now, and I'm amazed at how embedded it is in me, even though, as I say, I never dealt with it objectively before.

S.R.C. Do you think that we also contain racial instincts?

ARTHUR MILLER Yeah, I think so. I think that they're not racial instincts; that's kind of a gross way, a gross measure of it, calling it a racial instinct. There is a culture that is in gestures, in speech, in temperament, and in the reactions of one to another, which is certainly so basic that it is the first thing probably a kid, I think, is taught. And it goes right into the irrational of the unconscious before the child even gets asleep. We call this some kind of an ethnic or a racial inheritance. It doesn't matter, but I don't see how either one is saying that.

S.R.C. That's interesting in light of recent studies which seem to prove that a very young child is extremely sensitive to his surroundings.

ARTHUR MILLER Oh, I have no doubt about that, no doubt about it. See, it's an ingenuous example of schizophrenic people, of mothers especially who tend to have those traits even though they might not break down. They look in the bloodstream for it, and maybe sometimes it is there. But there is a certain schizophrenic reaction to life which the child is subjected to or lives with. They're going to have a schizophrenic frame of reference. I don't see how you can avoid that. That's how that damn thing, I think, gets carried on from generation to generation. For a part of them there is a question about the blood and how the blood can be a problem suddenly. But there is a predisposition as soon as that--excuse the term--mother starts to infect each child or reality. How is it avoided? Well, we can't avoid that.

S.R.C. Is that why Quentin says something to the effect that the sins of the father are handed down to the sons?

ARTHUR MILLER Yeah. There's a truth in it. It's true. The older one gets, the more of one's parents one recognizes in oneself. You'd think it would be the opposite; it isn't. The more purified it becomes, the more obvious it becomes.

S.R.C. In a lot of your works, you deal with guilt and seem to suggest that guilt can become a type of bad faith if it provides an individual with an excuse for not acting or taking his life into his own hands.

ARTHUR MILLER Yeah, it's a cop-out--guilt--in one sense if it doesn't mean anything underneath to that person. Guilt is not guilt if it is conscious. It is then something even more sinister. But I suppose the way I perceive it is that guilt is a sense of unusable responsibility; it's a responsibility that can't be expressed, that can't be utilized for one reason or another. On the other hand, it is a way of self-paralysis. It's a many-faceted thing. It's self-love, but I don't want to go on with a list of what it is. But it may be the most complicated phenomenon that a society embeds in its citizens. It's the consent that one gives to superior power. It's the way that we police ourselves in the name of the greater power. I could go on and on and on about what it consists of.

S.R.C. Would you say that at the end of *After the Fall*, Quentin transforms his guilt into responsibility?

ARTHUR MILLER He at least sees the need and feels the strength to attempt to do that, yeah.

S.R.C. The fact that he accepts Holga's love and then their movement off the stage together certainly seem to symbolize that transformation.

ARTHUR MILLER Yeah, right. See, I think, too, what is resented in that play is that he refuses to settle with being guilty. This is where most people stop, because if you don't stop there then you've got to act. It would have been far more palatable if he shot himself or jumped into the river with her. I would add that *After the Fall*, the title, is probably--I didn't think of it then, but I was very moved years earlier by *The Fall* by Camus. In Camus's *The Fall*, the man is guilty for not having acted to save a woman he never even saw or knew. And that's his fall. He recognizes all kinds of culpability, a species of responsibility, you might say, that was unacknowledged by his actions. And he's given up judging people, etc. The question in my play is what happens if you do go to the rescue. Does this absolve? Does this prevent the fall? Supposing he had run over to the bridge where he thought he heard someone fall in, and had become involved with her and found out that she had an inexorable lust for destruction, at what point and when would he see wisdom?

S.R.C. The point at which one says to himself: "Self-determinism--everyone has to be responsible for himself."

ARTHUR MILLER Exactly!

S.R.C. I saw the connection between these two works, but I never saw it in these terms before.

ARTHUR MILLER That's why it's *After the Fall.*

S.R.C. In *Incident at Vichy*, do you choose to have the prisoners face their interrogations alone to underscore, through their physical separation from each other, the fact that man must ultimately confront absurdity alone?

ARTHUR MILLER I hadn't thought of it in those terms. Actually, it was--what you say is true--but it is constructed that way because that's the way it was done in France.

S.R.C. The play has a symbolic movement.

ARTHUR MILLER Well, a lot of these things turn out to be symbolic--these symbolic bureaucratic processes that they invent. They do it instinctively; they're the great instinctive behavioral psychologists.

S.R.C. Do the white feathers that escape from the Old Jew's bag in *Incident at Vichy* symbolize ineffectual religions and value systems that make one take a passive or resigned posture in the face of his persecution?

ARTHUR MILLER I'll tell you that I didn't know myself what was in the bag, and that when I suddenly saw that they were feathers, it was totally out of some subconscious pocket in my mind. Then sometime later I saw a film, *The Shop on Main Street*, which is a Czech film, about a little town in Bohemia where all the Jews are rounded up. And they're told to bring a few things; they don't know where they're going, but they're going to their deaths, of course. They're loaded on the trucks, and the whole town is devastated; that is, it is emptied out of all the Jews that live in this town. And there's a shot of the town square where a little while ago we saw this crowd of people assembled and thrown into the vehicles. And what's blowing around on the square is the feathers. And this was a kind of a race memory of mine, quite frankly, because nothing like that ever happened in my family. My mother was born in this country; my father was brought over here at the age of six. But feathers--you see, you carry your bedding. It's the refugees' only possible property. It's light, it's warm, it's something he might sell if he had to, it's a touch of home, x,x,x,; it has all kinds of uses. And also it's the plumage of birds that are blown about. They're weak things--it does have an aspect of weakness, but also of domesticity, an uprooted domesticity. Then once they're released, you can't capture them any more. And there's a pathetic quality to that: the fact that the old guy's clutching what to our minds would be a practically valueless bag of nothing, or air. It's his identity, though. There's a lot of feed into that symbol.

S.R.C. I identified it with religious systems because he just sits there praying instead of doing anything actively to try to change his situation.

ARTHUR MILLER He's transcended it; he's got one foot in heaven. He knows that this is the ancient persecutor, the face of hell, that comes in every generation, and this is his turn with him. And it's been happening forever, and probably will go on happening forever. And he's praying against it. With one eye or the other, he's got his eye on God, who's reaching out His hands to him.

S.R.C. But is that an effective way of dealing with that type of crisis?

ARTHUR MILLER It's not effective; it's the last gasp of his limited range of possibilities.

S.R.C. You present a lot of different characters in that play who have their own ways of coping with that crisis.

ARTHUR MILLER That's right.

S.R.C. But only Von Berg, after being enlightened by Leduc, takes the action that turns things around and gives him a momentary triumph over his oppressors.

ARTHUR MILLER Yeah, right.

S.R.C. Doesn't a similar triumph occur in *Playing for Time*, when Fania Fenelon refuses to play in the orchestra unless her friend is allowed to join her?

ARTHUR MILLER Right. Well, she's pressing it to the limit there.

S.R.C. Isn't her survival itself another expression of her resistance to her persecutors?

ARTHUR MILLER Yeah, well I guess that story is the story of the survival of one who has a picked identity of herself. This is the survival of an alienated woman who knows she is alienated and has a vision of an unalienated world.

S.R.C. How about one last question? Would you agree that affirmation in your plays stems from the fact that the individual has the potential for the kind of self-determinism that is found in Proctor's resistance in *The Crucible* and Von Berg's actions in *Incident at Vichy*?

ARTHUR MILLER Absolutely! Yes, I think, incidentally, that what you choose to call optimism is interesting. See, it's interesting, isn't it, that I'm generally thought of as a pessimist, and I've always denied it, even though most of the time I feel pessimistic, personally. But I find that the more I investigate my own feelings, the less capable I am of conceding that in truth there is no hope to the extent that one logically should lie down and let evil triumph, because there is too much evidence that I see of the will to live. It's everywhere. Maybe it's because I've lived for twenty-five years out here where if you look around, life is just overwhelming. It is simply overwhelming. It's also in my relationship with children; one sees that struggle in the child, his wish to be taught. If the lesson of life was that we are helpless, we should have to teach children to breathe, and to struggle for hunger, to teach them to be hungry, to teach them to multiply; in other words, to awaken them to that tropism until death. But it's on the contrary. So you can see from that why I still have hope.

S.R.C. Thank you, Mr. Miller.

August 2, 1990

S.R.C. Do you think your drama has changed in any significant way from the earlier phases of your career to the more recent one that we have witnessed during the last decade or so?

ARTHUR MILLER Well, I suppose it has, but I really don't know how to define all of that. I think I started out far more intent on reaching a tragic form for our time; then my interest changed somewhat, and it turned more to a consideration of the question of what is real and what is illusory. I don't mean ideas necessarily. I don't mean real ideas and illusory ideas, but the quality of life that is a kind of cyclical repetitiousness in life that makes it seem less open to a storytelling motif. So I was really trying to deliver up this sense of life more than its tragic consequences, although in a work like *Playing for Time*, it's got a mixture of both things. I'm working on something now which is really a mixture of both.

S.R.C. But part of this sense of life you want to capture is the tragic?

ARTHUR MILLER Oh, definitely. Sure.

S.R.C. I asked that question because *Clara*, in particular, seems to have a very strong tragic sense.

ARTHUR MILLER It does. All of these things are questions of emphasis. They're not all that separate from each other. *Clara*, to me, is a perfectly traditional tragic play. It's just that its way of unveiling itself, or revealing itself, is somewhat untraditional.

S.R.C. Are you referring to the implosion of time in *Clara* which you have described in your autobiography, *Timebends*?

ARTHUR MILLER Yes, that's right.

S.R.C. There seems to be at least one noticeable difference between your earlier and later plays, and that has to do with how the tragic sense is conveyed. In the later plays, your characters reach an acceptance of their lives after experiencing some revelation, whereas in the earlier plays, the characters' inability to face themselves gives rise to the tragic consequences. Yet, perhaps ironically, the later plays often seem even more tragic because the characters live with some consciousness of their situation.

ARTHUR MILLER I think you've got something there. I think that it's reflecting something in our world now, in our society, in which we've had to live with what we know, instead of trying to deny what we know. We maybe deny a little less and shrug a little more.

S.R.C. When you explore the nature of reality in the later plays, you often seem to call everything into question. Are you suggesting that everything, even history, is subject to individual perception and interpretation?

ARTHUR MILLER Well, it can be. The only thing I would say about that is that there are still structures of what you could call moral view which lead us into suffering and death. The wages of sin is still death. If you still are working on illusions, the time may come more quickly when you have to confront the consequences for them. Consequences still exist. We've just managed to put them off for long periods of time. One obvious reference is the ecology. Everywhere in the world now is facing the consequences of the way we behave toward nature, toward our resources, toward each other. A city like London now is officially drinking poisoned water. I mean that's not a journalistic opinion. They've got stuff in there that they can never get out; it's poisoned the groundwater along the whole Thames valley. Well, you can disregard that for so long; it'll kill you finally. Look at what we did in Washington, with this United States Government lying to everybody all these years; on the economic front, the lying that went on in the Savings and Loan crisis. Birds do still come home to roost.

S.R.C. In essence, what you're saying is the individual is affected by the problems of society.

ARTHUR MILLER We're embedded in it, no doubt about it.

S.R.C. Yet even with such overwhelming forces operating beyond one's control, the individual still has to put up a struggle.

ARTHUR MILLER Well, he doesn't have to, but he has to if he wants to be connected with survival. Some people don't give a damn. You hear a lot of people saying, "Well, I've had forty years of life, so what the hell's the difference?" There's a lot of that, a lot of fatalistic surrender, more than I've ever known in my life. But it's very common now--you know, these rashes of outbreaks of teenage suicide in various parts of the country. I don't think that that's totally aberrant behavior. I think that there's something in the air that these kids caught a smell of.

S.R.C. But you would still say that even though definite limitations are placed upon them, people can make choices.

ARTHUR MILLER Oh, no doubt about it.

S.R.C. Your later plays explore fairly directly certain epistemological questions. In *The Archbishop's Ceiling*, for example, the characters seem intent on figuring out how they can know each other or their own reality while they must contend with the ambiguity that pervades their situation.

ARTHUR MILLER Yes, that's a fact.

S.R.C. Can the characters ever achieve any certainty about what they know?

ARTHUR MILLER They're pressing it as far as they can; they're trying as far as they can. They know what they can know, at least as far as I can imagine what they can know. But it could hardly be argued anymore that all we can know about man is only skimming the surface. I mean the news of the day, everyday, is some absolutely incongruous surprise about everything. You see when I refer to the political, as I often do in conversations, it's because it's so obvious it makes things clearer. When you consider that the CIA, funded by American money, has subsidized narcotics running out of Laos and Cambodia, and so on, while in the meantime, the other arm of the administration is trying to keep the stuff out of here, I mean what more do you need to say about the mystery of life!

S.R.C. Perhaps this context helps to explain why Adrian, the American in *The Archbishop's Ceiling*, loses faith in language? Doesn't he, too, realize that language--especially the official language of governments--is often just another web of deceit that prevents us from penetrating to the core of meaning?

ARTHUR MILLER Yes, that's correct.

S.R.C. A lot of the characters in your plays seem to be searching for an unalienated existence. But something always seems to prevent them from realizing their vision of themselves: in *The Archbishop's Ceiling* it is government oppression manifested in the characters' uncertainty over the microphone in the ceiling; in *Fame* it is Meyer's success; in *The American Clock* it is the Depression; in *Playing for Time* it is the Holocaust. Is it just a fact of life that we are alienated and the search for an unalienated existence is inevitable?

ARTHUR MILLER Sure.

S.R.C. Can the individual ever get a glimpse of that unalienated self?

ARTHUR MILLER Well, you know in one sense you can say every attempt at a governing philosophy is to circumvent alienation, or resolve it. The Christian idea is that if you believe sufficiently in Christ, you are at home; in another world, if not in this world, you know where you belong. The Marxist idea was that, by eliminating class struggle, ultimately man could be unalienated in his own house. The Buddhists and other religions do the same thing, I think. There's an old Southern or Western folk song, "Just Looking for a Home." Woody Guthrie used to sing it: "Just looking for a home, just looking for a home." He's speaking as much about bedbugs as anything else. All the creatures are looking for a home; they're trying to get out of the reach of danger--trying to survive. But so far, philosophically, we've just about failed, and there are still pockets in a society which seem to be a human habitat. But, after all, our police forces are getting larger and larger for good reason. There are more and more people who don't feel at home.

S.R.C. A lot of your characters seem to think they can find a home by clinging to their dreams, even when that means substituting lies for what is often an unbearable reality. Yet in *The American Clock*, the dreams kindle hope, a hope beyond despair, whereas in many of your other plays self-delusion is very destructive.

ARTHUR MILLER Well there's a difference--I hope there's a difference--between hope and self-delusion. Or maybe it will turn out, if we all go down poisoned, that there was no difference. I persist in thinking that there is; that there is far more that we could do to make a home of this world than we are doing--by acting responsibly, and so forth. But a lot of these plays are simply examining the common condition, at least the psychological condition as people feel it on their skins.

S.R.C. So the dream for a better world does not necessarily have to be an illusion?

ARTHUR MILLER No. Without that hope, let's face it, a lot of things should be able to change. You see we're now down to a half-drugged society. I sometimes think that the main occupation of the country is supplying an addictive population with drugs and trying to prevent them from shooting each other, or themselves, or us. And that's some aspect of this whole discussion: are they finding hope in drugs or are they simply signing off? Some say one thing; some say another. It's sort of a religion with one parishioner.

S.R.C. Your characters have different ways of finding hope. In *I Can't Remember Anything*, for example, Leonora takes comfort from nature, but she does not seem to be conscious of its effect on her.

ARTHUR MILLER Well, she is that way as a character. It's obscure in her, but it's the only thing keeping her sane. But then

she can still look out the window and see these natural things--
the trees and the deer and the grass--and they remind her of life.
But there's no ideology behind that. What's difficult for me to
convey is that I really start with characters with the way they are
and try to confront what their implications are, philosophically,
rather than arrive at a philosophical point and then construct a
play around it. I might have been better off had I done that; it
would have been much easier for people to approach.

S.R.C. That play works so well because the two characters are
highly individuated with completely different orientations toward
life. It is clear from the start that conflict between them is
inevitable. Are we meant to see her dance at the end as an
acceptance of her life?

ARTHUR MILLER Yes, you should. That's exactly what should
have happened.

S.R.C. And we learn from Leo, who never seems to lose touch
with reality, that life is what it is; we just simply have to live it.

ARTHUR MILLER That's right. That's exactly the way it
should be.

S.R.C. With your creation of such highly individuated and
memorable characters, it is impossible not to notice the tremendous value you place on individuality. Do you think this
emphasis has anything to do with your being an American
playwright? Is it a cultural inheritance--this emphasis on indi-
viduality--derived in part from some aspect of the American
Dream?

ARTHUR MILLER It possibly is in my case, but, of course,
other people in other countries share this same idea, even if they
express it differently. We've got that damn phrase, the American
Dream, which nobody's been able to define. When *Death of a*

Salesman went on in Beijing, one of the young men coming out of the theater was interviewed by CBS. I saw it on camera. Now he had no indoctrination about this play at all. They had never heard of this play. And he said, "Well, Willy's right. Everybody does want to be number one. And Biff is wrong; he shouldn't be at his father for wanting that for him. Everybody wants his son to excel." And I was sitting there listening and I thought he was speaking completely like a man from Mars, simply looking at the evidence, not from his own life. After all, he looked to me about twenty or in his early twenties, so he's younger than the Chinese Revolution. And he's been brought up in a community where communal values were *the* values and individualism was a curse. So it makes you smile. We can only begin to grin at the pretensions we all have at having some final construction, some final answer.

S.R.C. You seem to be suggesting that the movement toward individual identity is something like an archetypal pattern--something experienced in most cultures. It isn't American only; it is universal and all societies experience it.

ARTHUR MILLER I think it is. I'm sure it is. I think it's everywhere. We made a fetish out of the whole thing. We advertise ourselves that way.

S.R.C. In *The Archbishop's Ceiling*, where we see an American interacting with Europeans, it is obvious that the American refuses to relinquish his hope while the others have embraced despair as a way of life. With the contrast of these characters and their different cultural viewpoints, isn't there some suggestion of an American insistence on possibility?

ARTHUR MILLER Well, there again it's less a philosophical statement than a dramatic contrast. He, Adrian, finds it intolerable that anybody should tell him what to do about anything. Well, of course, in Europe, people have been telling other people what to do for centuries. On the one hand, they see the American as a bit of a child. It's part of our childishness. You see, the child wants also to be rid of his parental guidance. They know that it is impossible, that the state is a power structure; its job is to control people. The other ones, the Europeans, are very alike. But there's something precious about him, too, in all his naivete. If the world loses what he's demanding, it's all gone. We would simply end up a beehive.

S.R.C. Perhaps it is more evident in *The Archbishop's Ceiling* than elsewhere, but the significance of power is another motif that is found repeatedly in your later work. Oftentimes, the struggle for power involves the characters' struggle to control how they are perceived by others. While this desire is usually associated with personal self-interest, on at least one occasion, in *Playing for Time*, it is a way of preserving one's dignity and self-esteem.

ARTHUR MILLER Yes, that's the way it goes.

S.R.C. So sometimes it is acceptable to desire power?

ARTHUR MILLER Well, sometimes you have to want it because you're in an intolerable situation under the power of others, then you have a revolution, which can't be argued with. You know, when things get intolerable, people get an obligation to overthrow them. We certainly did that in this country. And, of course, this has happened in normal times elsewhere. I mean there's no arguing with this, whether you think it's a good idea or it isn't. It's a fact of life. It's like arguing with a storm.

S.R.C. Even when they are not trying to control others by manipulating their perceptions, the characters in your later plays, especially in *The Archbishop's Ceiling, Elegy for a Lady*, and *Some Kind of Love Story*, seem desperately to need to talk. Is talking for some of these characters a way of defining their reality?

ARTHUR MILLER You know, in the beginning was the word, says the Bible. They're trying to name themselves; they're trying to define themselves because the moral situation is so nebulous and few people can ever know what side they're on, or if there are sides. So they talk themselves into positions.

S.R.C. That strikes me as a very good way of describing what happens to the Man in *Elegy for a Lady*. Even the structure of the play calls attention to his effort to engage in the kind of dialogue that will help him to define his feelings.

ARTHUR MILLER Yes. It's a monologue, in effect. He's trying to figure himself out and what his nature is. I guess they do talk themselves into it.

S.R.C. If you could boil it down to just a single thing, what would you say is the one effect you most wanted to achieve in your later plays?

ARTHUR MILLER My interest really is to try to capture some of the smell and sense of this very vagrant thing we call existence, and that's most difficult.

Summary of Arthur Miller's Major Works

The Man Who Had All the Luck (1944)

Miller's first Broadway play was not received well by the New York theater critics. The play tells the story of a young man, David Frieber, who has a difficult time coping with success. According to Miller, Frieber is convinced that it is "a law of life . . . that people are always frustrated in some important regard." Having been fortunate in love, in fatherhood, and in his career, David lives in fear of some "impending disaster." To relieve his anxiety, he deliberately sets in motion the process that ultimately destroys his business. Ironically, Miller suggests all the time that David alone is responsible for his destiny--a fact David can appreciate only after he suffers financial ruin.

Focus (1945)

A man who had discriminated against Jews ironically finds himself the victim of Anti-Semitism. After he dons a pair of eyeglasses that transform his physical appearance, Lawrence Newman, the novel's central character, discovers how easy it is for anyone to become the target of ridicule and aggression. Mistakenly identifying Newman as a Jew, former friends and acquaintances turn against him and treat him with hostility. He eventually loses his job and faces the same discrimination in his job search that he had previously exercised in his treatment of ethnic minorities. At the end, after helping his Jewish neighbor survive a brutal street attack, Newman refuses to correct a police officer's misrepresentation of him as a Jew. By accepting his connection to the Jews, Newman demonstrates his willingness to accept responsibility for all others.

All My Sons (1947)

Winner of the New York Drama Critics' Circle Award, this play considers the effects of war profiteering on a family and its society. The central character, Joe Keller, is a successful businessman who keeps his company from bankruptcy by selling defective airplane parts to the army during the Second World War. When twenty-one pilots die because of the faulty engines, Keller is arrested and tried for the crime. Letting his partner take the blame for his unethical business practices, Keller is exonerated by the courts but is later condemned by his son, Chris, when he discovers his father's guilt. Having watched his troops selflessly die for each other in combat, Chris rejects Keller's justification of his crime--that anything is permissible to save the family--and eventually forces his father to admit his guilt and social responsibility.

Death of a Salesman (1949)

Universally celebrated as Miller's masterpiece, this riveting play about the Loman family's struggle for love and understanding won a Pulitzer Prize. The central character, Willy Loman, is an aging traveling salesman who, after years of devoted service, loses his job because he has become an embarrassment to his company. Tormented by the fear that his life is a lie, and haunted by the guilt that stems from his son's discovery of his infidelity, the mentally exhausted salesman can no longer stop his mind from drifting back to remembrances of a romanticized past. The mobile concurrency of past and present in Willy's mind eventually coalesces and brings him into direct confrontation with his role in his family's demise. Rather than face his shame by acknowledging the truth of his dishonest existence, Willy takes refuge in a desperate act of suicide. His death is his final act of bad faith, for Willy tries to deceive himself into believing that his suicide will retrieve his family's love and his lost honor. Sadly, it wins him neither.

An Enemy of the People (1950)

Miller's adaptation of Ibsen's play sticks fairly closely to the original. The play tells the story of a respected doctor who finds himself ostracized from his society when he opposes his town's decision to conceal a report that the springs, a major tourist attraction and source of revenue, are polluted and pose a risk to the public's health. The idealistic Dr. Stockmann resists society's pressure to conform and finds himself branded an enemy of the people at the play's close.

The Crucible (1953)

Usually regarded as an allegory of the McCarthy red baiting and purging that occurred in America after World War II, this play recreates the harrowing Salem Witchcraft Trials of 1692. Playing upon their elders' fears and prejudices, several mischievous and sexually repressed young girls accuse innocent townspeople of witchcraft. At first, the accused consist mostly of the less respectable members of society, but eventually the town's leading landowners are among the indicted and persecuted. The action intensifies when the central character, John Proctor, must publicly confess his adultery and denounce his mistress to save his wife, who has been accused of witchcraft by his lover. After an eerie courtroom scene, in which the girls denounce their victims and Proctor attempts, but fails, to break their hold over the court, he faces his most severe crisis of conscience when he is given the chance to secure his freedom by denouncing his friends as witches. Choosing to die rather than destroy the reputation of innocent people, Proctor stands tall in Miller's canon as a model of human conduct.

A Memory of Two Mondays (1955)

This nostalgic one-act play is a gentle remembrance of life during the Depression. Based in part on Miller's own experiences working in an automobile parts warehouse in the days before he went away to college, this play takes a wistful look at the various people he met who face life with a feeling of helplessness and hopelessness. The bittersweet tenderness pervading the play helps to convey the impression that one must feel compassion at the misfortune of others.

A View from the Bridge (1956)

The expanded two-act version is a powerful play. It tells the story of a sexually repressed dock worker who commits an act of betrayal in his community that results in his irremediable alienation. Incapable of having his views challenged by others, Eddie Carbone fails to admit that his illicit desire for his niece fuels the jealousy he feels when a young illegal immigrant asks for her hand in marriage. After reporting the aliens to immigration authorities, and thereby breaking faith with his community, Carbone projects his guilt onto others and refuses to accept responsibility for his actions. Rather than face his real motives for betraying the immigrants, he challenges the older alien to a fatal street fight to win back his tarnished name and dies without ever recognizing the role he played in his own destruction.

The Misfits (1961)

Written as a token of love for his second wife, Marilyn Monroe, this screenplay creates a striking metaphor for the human condition. The movie tells the story of a couple of modern-day cowboys who refuse to settle down and live a conventional life in society. Lost in a world that no longer respects the values and traditions of the past, the cowboys use alcohol, casual sex, and reckless rodeo antics to conceal their disillusionment. A furious mustang chase, however, forces them to evaluate their lives and admit the futility of their effort to recapture the past. They eventually acknowledge that times have changed and that the mustangs, once a favorite among young children, are now butchered for dog food. One cowboy, however, discovers that meaning can be restored to existence. His personal salvation takes the shapely form of a beautiful divorcee with an insatiable appetite for life and love of all living creatures. With her guidance, he learns how to express his feelings and, comforted by each other's love, they find the courage to face their uncertain future together.

After the Fall (1964)

A highly autobiographical play that received rough treatment from the critics for Miller's public dramatization of episodes from his turbulent marriage to Marilyn Monroe, *After the Fall* is a provocative work that examines the relation between public and private acts of betrayal and cruelty and questions whether love is enough to save human beings from their own destructive tendencies. While centering his drama around one man's introspective self-evaluation, Miller frequently draws parallels between private acts of betrayal in his central character's life and public atrocities committed during the Holocaust. In linking these two levels of the play, Miller suggests that the will to power and instinct for self-preservation are too strong for love alone to ensure humanity's survival.

Incident at Vichy (1964)

A companion piece to *After the Fall*, *Incident at Vichy* is set in France in 1942 during the German occupation. The play investigates the underlying reasons for the anti-Semitism that resulted in the atrocities of the Holocaust during the Second World War. A group of prisoners awaiting interrogation discuss their feelings about the occupation, the resistance, and anti-Semitism in Europe at the time. After several rousing debates and a few intense moments of confrontation with their captors, an Austrian Prince, who has been given his pass to freedom, makes a noble sacrifice by handing his pass over to a Jewish psychiatrist, Leduc. By transforming guilt into responsibility, Von Berg shows that, even in the most absurd of situations, one can choose to give meaning and dignity to human existence.

The Price (1968)

This largely unknown, but highly effective, play looks at the internal and external conflicts that develop when two middle-aged brothers meet to divide their deceased father's belongings. The two men have chosen markedly different paths in life: one is a successful and prosperous surgeon while the other is an underpaid policeman. As the play progresses, it becomes clear that each brother resents the other, one because of the other's financial prosperity, the other because of his brother's strong family ties. The tension between the two leads to a rousing confrontation, where each man is faced with the choices of his past and must decide whether to accept or renounce his life. The argument between the brothers is arbitrated by one of Miller's most delightful characters, a ninety-year-old furniture dealer who delivers some of Miller's best comic lines.

The Creation of the World and Other Business (1972)

Based on the Biblical story of Adam and Eve's fall from grace in the Garden of Eden, this play represents Miller's first sustained exploration of the comic mode. Often whimsical, at times irreverent, but always amusing, this comedy uses the story of the fall to trace the origin of consciousness in human beings and explore certain metaphysical issues--such as the nature of good and evil--that are frequently the subject of Miller's other plays. A couple of years after its initial Broadway production, this play was turned into a musical called *Up from Paradise* (1974).

The Archbishop's Ceiling (1977)

Set in an Eastern European communist bloc city during the Cold War, this play considers the effect of oppression on personal identity, human relations, and artistic expression. A group of writers sitting in a room suspect that microphones planted by the government are concealed in the ceiling. No one knows for certain that the microphones exist, but the suspicion that they may be there drastically affects everyone's speech and behavior. In essence, the writers perform for each other and the hidden power symbolized by the archbishop's ceiling. According to Miller, the play becomes "a dramatic meditation on the impact of immense state power upon human identity and the common concept of what is real and illusory."

Fame (1978)

A successful playwright suffers an identity crisis as he attempts to reconcile his newly won public image with his private existence. His extreme self-consciousness of his situation leaves him feeling alienated and disoriented until he has a chance encounter with a homely female jockey. She helps him learn how to transcend appearances in order to discover the truth of his personal reality.

The American Clock (1980)

The personal tragedies that accompanied the Great Depression in America during the 1930s inspired the dramatic action in this play. Combining the expansiveness of the epic with the humor of vaudeville, this play gives a panoramic view of the country's reaction to the Depression without losing sight of the intense personal crisis experienced in the individual family household. While the play is often tragic in tone, a spirit of hopefulness pervades the piece--thanks in large measure to the atmosphere created by Miller's inclusion of numerous romantic musical scores from the period.

Playing for Time (1980)

Adapted from Fania Fenelon's memoir, Miller's highly acclaimed screenplay tells the remarkable story of one courageous woman who survived the Holocaust at Auschwitz. In the midst of a nightmarish landscape of human suffering and depravity, Fania Fenelon faces the ultimate challenge to her dignity and proves that nothing--not even the threat of death--can force the individual to act ignobly or relinquish her sense of responsibility.

Elegy for a Lady (1980)

A man who enters a boutique to buy a gift for his dying mistress discovers much about himself and his lover. Through his conversation with the boutique's proprietress, the man learns that he may have misunderstood his lover's feelings toward their relationship. The proprietress also leads him to a better understanding of his motives in ending his relationship with his mistress and eventually helps him to preserve a lasting memory of a special, but not deep, friendship. What makes the play fascinating is its ambiguity. Questions about the strange relationship between the man and the proprietress are never fully answered and prompt philosophical speculations about the elusive nature of reality.

Some Kind of Love Story (1982)

Set in a New England town where an innocent man has been imprisoned for the murder of his uncle, this play looks at the personal conflict experienced by a detective who attempts to draw out the testimony from the only witness who can free his client. What complicates his task is the fact that his witness is a schizophrenic with bizarre multiple personalities who is liable at any moment to confuse fantasy with reality. Her personality shifts keep the detective (and the audience) in doubt about the reliability of her evidence. His struggle to wrest vital information from her, while desperately attempting to distinguish fact from fiction, reality from appearance, meshes nicely with the taut social drama involving political corruption. This one-act play was subsequently expanded and made into a movie entitled *Everybody Wins* (1990).

I Can't Remember Anything (1987)

Two elderly friends dining together discuss their conflicting views of life and the significance of their memories. The woman, Leonora, suffers from severe depression and sees herself as totally useless. As the play progresses and they enjoy shared remembrances of special friendships with deceased loved ones, Leonora comes to appreciate the meaning of her life and gains the strength she needs to face her own mortality.

Clara (1987)

A detective arrives at the scene of a brutal murder and tries to solve the crime by piecing together the fragmentary clues extracted from the victim's father, Albert Kroll. As the interrogation proceeds, Kroll is thrust back to scenes from his past that indict him for instilling liberal values in his daughter that may have indirectly led to her death. As a result of several key revelations, Kroll comes to accept his culpability without abandoning his commitment to social responsibility. He chooses to embrace his life even though he knows that doing so necessitates accepting the tragedy of Clara's sacrifice.

The Last Yankee (1991)

Two men from different backgrounds discuss their similar situations in the waiting room of a state hospital. As the men attempt to understand the reasons for their wives' mental problems, their conversation turns into an argument about their own personal differences in outlook and life styles. At the end, nothing is resolved between them; they remain incomprehensible to each other even though they share an unspoken anxiety about their wives' condition.

The Ride Down Mount Morgan (1991)

This provocative, and often hilarious, play tells the story of Lyman Felt, a bigamist recovering from a car accident who suddenly learns that a confrontation over his infidelity with his two wives is imminent. As key episodes from the past are merged with actual and imagined scenes in the present, Lyman tries to convince himself--and his two families--that everyone has benefitted from his duplicity. In spite of his wives' angry recriminations and denunciations, Lyman refuses to admit that his life has been a cleverly orchestrated lie. He futilely embraces self-delusion as a way of escaping from his unpleasant situation, only to find himself abandoned and scorned by both wives at the play's end.

Selected Bibliography

Books:

After the Fall. New York: Viking, 1964.
    (periodical edition) *Saturday Evening Post* 237 (February 1, 1964): 24-59.
    (revised stage version) New York: Viking, 1964, 1965. London: Secker & Warburg, 1965.
    (paperback edition, revised stage version) New York: Bantam, 1965.
    (acting edition, revised stage version) New York: Dramatists Play Service, 1965.
    (paperback edition, revised stage version) New York: Compass, 1968.
    (paperback edition, television adaptation) New York: Bantam, 1974.
    (paperback edition, revised stage version) New York: Penguin, 1978.
All My Sons. New York: Reynal & Hitchcock, 1947.
    (acting edition) New York: Dramatists Play Service, 1947. Harmondsworth: Penguin, 1961.
The American Clock (acting edition) New York: Dramatists Play Service, 1982.
    London: Methuen, 1983.

(revised stage version) New York: Grove, 1989.

The Archbishop's Ceiling (revised stage version). London: Methuen, 1984.

(revised stage version) New York: Grove, 1989.

Arthur Miller's Collected Plays. Vol. 1. New York: Viking, 1957. Contains *All My Sons, Death of a Salesman, The Crucible, A Memory of Two Mondays,* and *A View from the Bridge* (two-act version).

Arthur Miller's Collected Plays. Vol. 2. New York: Viking, 1981. Contains *The Misfits* (cinema-novel), *After the Fall, Incident at Vichy, The Price, The Creation of the World and Other Business,* and *Playing for Time* (adaptation, screenplay).

Chinese Encounters (reportage). New York: Farrar, Straus and Giroux, 1979.

Conversations with Arthur Miller (interviews). Ed. Matthew C. Roudane. Jackson: University Press of Mississippi, 1987.

The Creation of the World and Other Business. New York: Viking, 1973.

(acting edition) New York: Dramatists Play Service, 1973. London: Secker and Warburg, 1981.

The Crucible. New York: Viking, 1953.

(periodical edition) *Theatre Arts* 37 (October, 1953): 35-67.

(acting edition) New York: Dramatists Play Service, 1954. London: Cresset, 1956.

(paperback edition) New York: Bantam, 1959.

(paperback edition) New York: Compass, 1964.

(text and criticism) Ed. Gerald Weales. New York: Viking, 1971.

(paperback edition) New York: Penguin, 1976.

Danger: Memory! New York: Grove, 1986.

Contains *I Can't Remember Anything* and *Clara.* London: Methuen, 1986.

Death of a Salesman. New York: Viking, 1949. London: Cresset, 1949.

(periodical edition) *Theatre Arts* 35 (March, 1951): 49-91.

(paperback edition) New York: Bantam, 1951, 1955.

(acting edition) New York: Dramatists Play Service, 1952.

(paperback edition) New York: Compass, 1958.

London: Harmondsworth: Penguin, 1961.

(text and criticism) Ed. Gerald Weales. New York: Viking, 1967.

(paperback edition) New York: Penguin, 1976.

Elegy for a Lady (periodical edition). *Esquire* 94 (December,1980): 98-104.

(acting edition) New York: Dramatists Play Service, 1982.

An Enemy of the People (adaptation). New York: Viking, 1951.

(acting edition) New York: Dramatists Play Service, 1951.

(paperback edition) Harmondsworth: Penguin, 1977.

Everybody Wins (screenplay). New York: Grove, 1990.

Focus (novel). New York: Reynal & Hitchcock, 1945.

London: Gollancz, 1949.

(paperback edition) New York: Dell, 1959.

(paperback edition) New York: Penguin, 1978.

The Golden Years. London: Methuen, 1989.

I Don't Need You Any More: Stories (short fiction). New York: Viking, 1967.

London: Secker and Warburg, 1967.

Incident at Vichy. New York: Viking, 1965.

(acting edition) New York: Dramatists Play Service, 1966.

London: Secker and Warburg, 1966.

(paperback edition) New York: Bantam, 1967.

(paperback edition) New York: Penguin, 1978.

London: Secker and Warburg, 1981.

In the Country (reportage). New York: Viking, 1977.

In Russia (reportage). New York: Viking, 1969.

London: Secker and Warburg, 1969.

Jane's Blanket (children's story). New York: Crowell/Collier, 1963.

London: Collier/Macmillan, 1963.

The Last Yankee (acting edition). New York: Dramatists Play
Service, 1991.
The Man Who Had All the Luck. In *Cross-Section: A Collection of
New American Writing*. Ed. Edwin Seaver. New
York: Fischer, 1944: 486-552.
(revised stage version) London: Methuen, 1989.
A Memory of Two Mondays. In *A View from the Bridge: Two One-
Act Plays*. New York: Viking, 1955.
(acting edition) New York: Dramatists Play Service, 1956.
(periodical edition) *Theatre Arts* 40 (September 1956):
33-68.
London: Cresset, 1960.
The Misfits (cinema-novel). New York: Viking, 1961.
(paperback edition) New York: Dell, 1961.
London: Secker and Warburg, 1961.
(paperback edition, final shooting script) In *Film Scripts
Three*. Ed. George P. Garrett. New York: Apple-
ton-Century-Crofts, 1972: 202-382.
"The Misfits" and Other Stories (short fiction). New York: Scrib-
ner's, 1987.
Playing for Time (adaptation, screenplay). New York: Bantam,
1981.
(acting edition) Chicago: Dramatic Publishing Compa-
ny, 1985.
Plays. Vol. 1. London: Methuen, 1988.
Contains *All My Sons, Death of a Salesman, The Crucible,
A Memory of Two Mondays*, and *A View from the Bridge*
(two-act version).
Plays. Vol. 2. London: Methuen, 1988.
Contains *The Misfits* (cinema-novel), *After the Fall, Inci-
dent at Vichy, The Price, The Creation of the World and
Other Business*, and *Playing for Time* (adaptation, screen-
play).
Plays. Vol. 3. London: Methuen, 1990.

Contains *The American Clock*, *The Archbishop's Ceiling*, and *Two-Way Mirror* (a collection of the two one-act plays, *Elegy for a Lady* and *Some Kind of Love Story*).

The Portable Arthur Miller. Ed. Harold Clurman. New York: Penguin, 1977.
Contains *Death of a Salesman*, *The Crucible*, *Incident at Vichy*, *The Price*, and shorter works.

The Price. New York: Viking, 1968.
London: Secker and Warburg, 1968.
(periodical edition, condensed version) *Saturday Evening Post* 241 (February 10, 1968): 40-59.
(acting edition) New York: Dramatists Play Service, 1968.
(paperback edition) New York: Bantam, 1969.
(paperback edition) New York: Penguin, 1978.
London: Secker and Warburg, 1981.

The Ride Down Mount Morgan. London: Methuen, 1991.
(revised stage version) New York: Penguin, 1992.

"Salesman" in Beijing (memoir). New York: Viking, 1984.
London: Methuen, 1984.

Situation Normal (reportage). New York: Reynal & Hitchcock, 1944.

Some Kind of Love Story (acting edition). New York: Dramatists Play Service, 1983.

The Theater Essays of Arthur Miller (drama criticism). Ed. Robert A. Martin. New York: Viking, 1978.
(paperback edition). Harmondsworth: Penguin, 1978.
London: Secker and Warburg, 1979.

Timebends: A Life (autobiography). New York, Grove, 1987.

Two-Way Mirror: A Double-bill. London: Methuen, 1984.
Contains two one-act plays, *Elegy for a Lady* and *Some Kind of Love Story*.

A View from the Bridge (one-act version). In *A View from the Bridge: Two One-Act Plays*. New York: Viking, 1955.
London: Cresset, 1957.

A View from the Bridge: A Play in Two Acts (acting edition).
New York: Dramatists Play Service, 1957.
London: Cresset, 1957.
(paperback edition) Harmondsworth: Penguin, 1961.
Up from Paradise (acting edition). New York: French, 1984.

Minor Plays:
Grandpa and the Statue. In *Radio Drama in Action.* Ed. Erik Bar-
nouw. New York: Farrar and Rinehart, 1945: 265-281.
The Guardsman (adaptation). In *Theatre Guild on the Air.* Ed.
H. William Fitelson. New York: Rinehart, 1947: 69-97.
The Pussycat and the Expert Plumber Who Was a Man. In *One
Hundred Non-Royalty Radio Plays.* Ed. William Kozlen-
ko. New York: Greenberg, 1941: 20-30.
The Story of Gus. In *Radio's Best Plays.* Ed. Joseph Liss. New
York: Greenberg, 1947: 303-319.
That They May Win. In *The Best One-Act Plays of 1944.* Ed. Mar-
garet Mayorga. New York: Dodd and Mead, 1945: 45-60.
Three Men on a Horse (adaptation). In *Theatre Guild on the Air.*
Ed. H. William Fitelson. New York: Rinehart, 1947:
207-238.
*William Ireland's Confession. In One Hundred Non-Royalty
Plays.* Ed. William Kozlenko. New York: Greenberg,
1941: 512-521.

Unpublished Plays (listed chronologically):

No Villain, 1936. Microfilm copy, Harlan Hatcher Library,
University of Michigan.
They Too Arise (revised version of *No Villain*), 1936. Typescript
in the New York Public Library.
Honors at Dawn, 1937. Microfilm copy, Harlan Hatcher Li-
brary, University of Michigan.
The Great Disobedience, 1938. Typescript in the Harlan Hatcher
Library, University of Michigan.
The Grass Still Grows (revised version of *They Too Arise*), 1939.

Typescripts in the Humanities Research Center, University of Texas, and the Harlan Hatcher Library, University of Michigan.

Listen My Children (written with Norman Rosten), 1939. Typescript in the Library of Congress.

The Golden Years (unpublished version), 1939-40. Typescript in the Humanities Research Center, University of Texas.

The Four Freedoms (radio play), 1942. Typescript in the Library of Congress.

The Half-Bridge, 1941-43. Typescript in the Humanities Research Center, University of Texas.

The Hook (screenplay), 1951. Typescript in the Humanities Research Center, University of Texas.

Prose Fiction and Poetry (listed chronologically):

"It Takes a Thief." *Collier's* 119 (February 1947): 23, 75-76.

"Bridge to a Savage World" (unfinished screenplay). *Esquire* 50 (October 1958): 185-190.

"Lines from California" (poem). *Harper's* 238 (May 1969): 97.

"Rain in a Strange City" (prose poem). *Travel & Leisure* 4 (September 1974): 8.

"Ham Sandwich." *Boston University Journal* 24 (1976): 5-6.

"The Poosidin's Resignation" (a play fragment). *Boston University Journal* 24 (1976): 7-13.

"White Puppies." *Esquire* 90 (July 1978): 32-36.

"1928 Buick." *Atlantic* 242 (October 1978): 49-51.

"Homely Girl." *Grand Street* (forthcoming).

Interviews:

Allsop, Kenneth. "A Conversation with Arthur Miller." *Encounter* 13 (July 1959): 58-60.

"Arthur Miller Ad-Libs on Elia Kazan." *Show* (January 1964): 55-56.

"Arthur Miller on *The Crucible*." *Audience* 2 (July-August 1972): 46-47.

"Arthur Miller Talks." *Michigan Quarterly Review* 6 (Summer 1967): 153-184.

Atlas, James. "The Creative Journey of Arthur Miller Leads Back to Broadway and TV." *New York Times*, 28 September 1980, Sec. 2, pp. 1, 32.

Balakian, Janet. "A Conversation with Arthur Miller." *Michigan Quarterly Review* 29 (Spring 1990): 158-170.

____. "An Interview with Arthur Miller." *Studies in American Drama, 1945-Present* 6 (1991): 29-47.

Barthel, Joan. "Arthur Miller Ponders *The Price*." *New York Times*, 28 January 1968, Sec. 2, pp. 1, 5.

Bigsby, Christopher. *Arthur Miller and Company*. London: Methuen, 1990.

____. "Miller's Odyssey to a Brutal Decade." *Guardian*, 4 August 1986, p. 9.

Brandon, Henry. "The State of the Theater: A Conversation with Arthur Miller and Marilyn Monroe." *Harper's* 221 (November 1960): 63-69.

Buckley, Tom. "Miller Takes His Comedy Seriously." *New York Times*, 29 August 1972, p. 22.

Calta, Louis. "Miller Defends Theme of *Price*." *New York Times*, 5 March 1968, p. 32.

Carlisle, Olga and Rose Styron. "The Art of the Theater II: Arthur Miller, An Interview." *Paris Review* 10 (Summer 1966): 61-98.

Carroll, James and Helen Epstein. "Seeing Eye to Eye." *Boston Review* 14 (February 1989): 12-13.

Centola, Steven R. "'Just Looking for a Home': A Conversation with Arthur Miller." *American Drama* 1 (Fall 1991): 85-94.

____. "'The Will to Live': An Interview with Arthur Miller." *Modern Drama* 27 (September 1984): 345-360.

Christiansen, Richard. "Arthur Miller's Verdict on Willy: He Has Elements of Nobility." *Chicago Tribune*, 15 January 1984, Sec. 13, p. 19.

____. "Dustin Hoffman and the Rebirth of a Classic *Salesman*." *Chicago Tribune*, 15 January 1984, Sec. 13, p. 18.

"The Contemporary Theater." *Michigan Quarterly Review* 6 (Summer 1967): 153-163.

"Conversation at St. Clerans between Arthur Miller and John Huston." *Guardian*, 25 February 1960, p. 6.

Cook, Jim. "Their Thirteenth Year Was Most Significant." *Washington Post and Times Herald*, 10 July 1956, p. 24.

Corrigan, Robert W. "Arthur Miller: Interview." *Michigan Quarterly Review* 13 (Autumn 1974): 401-405.

Downer, Alan. "Mr. Williams and Mr. Miller." *Furioso* 4 (Summer 1949): 66-70.

Evans, Richard. *Psychology and Arthur Miller*. New York: Dutton, 1969.

Fallaci, Oriana. "A Propos of *After the Fall*." *World Theatre* 14 (January 1965): 79, 81.

Feldman, Robert. "Arthur Miller on the Theme of Evil: An Interview." *Resources for American Literary Study* 17 (Spring 1990): 87-93.

Feron, James. "Miller in London to See *Crucible*." *New York Times*, 24 January 1965, p. 82.

Frank, Stanley. "A Playwright Ponders a New Outline for TV." *TV Guide, 8 October 1966, pp. 7-8, 10-11.*

"Freedom in the Mass Media." Michigan Quarterly Review 6 (Summer 1967): 163-178.

Funke, Lewis. "Stars Help Arthur Miller Film TV Antiwar Allegory." *New York Times*, 17 November 1969, p. 58.

____. "Thoughts on a Train Bound for Wilmington." *New York Times*, 18 January 1953, pp. 1, 3.

____. "A Zestful Miller Starts Rehearsal." *New York Times*, 6 December 1967, p. 40.

Gelb, Barbara. "Question: 'Am I my Brother's Keeper?'" *New York Times*, 29 November 1964, Sec. 2, pp. 1, 3.

Gelb, Phillip. "*Death of a Salesman*: A Symposium." Tulane Drama Review 2 (May 1958): 63-69.

___. "Morality and Modern Drama." *Educational Theatre Journal* 10 (October 1958): 190-202.

Gilroy, Harry. "A Million Sales for Willy Loman." *New York Times*, 8 March 1968, p. 36.

Gollub, Christian-Albrecht. "Interview with Arthur Miller." *Michigan Quarterly Review* 16 (Spring 1977): 121-141.

Goode, James. *The Making of The Misfits.* New York: Limelight Editions, 1986.

Goyen, William. "Arthur Miller's Quest for Truth." *New York Herald-Tribune Magazine*, 19 January 1964, p. 35.

Greenfield, Josh. "'Writing Plays Is Absolutely Senseless, Arthur Miller Says, 'But I love It. I Just Love It.'" *New York Times Magazine*, 13 February 1972, pp. 16-17, 34-39.

Griffin, John and Alice. "Arthur Miller Discusses *The Crucible.*" *Theater Arts* 37 (October 1953): 33-34.

Gruen, Joseph. "Portrait of a Playwright at Fifty." *New York* 24 October 1965: 12-13.

Guo, Jide. "My Interview with Arthur Miller." *Foreign Literatures* 5 (1987): 31-38.

Gussow, Mel. "Arthur Miller Returns to Genesis for First Musical." *New York Times*, 17 April 1974, p. 37.

___. "Arthur Miller: Stirred by Memory." *New York Times*, 1 February 1987, Sec. 2, pp. 1, 30.

Halberstam, David. "Polish Students Question Miller." *New York Times*, 17 February 1965, p. 36.

Hayman, Ronald. "Arthur Miller." *Playback II.* London: Davis-Poynter, 1973: 7-22.

___. "Interview with Arthur Miller." *Arthur Miller.* London: Heinemann, 1970: 1-14.

Heaton, C. P. "Arthur Miller on *Death of a Salesman.*" *Notes on Contemporary Literature* 1 (1971): 5.

Hewes, Henry. "Broadway Postscript: Arthur Miller and How He Went to the Devil." *Saturday Review* 31 January 1953: 24-26.

___. "Death of a Longshoreman." *Saturday Review* 15 October 1955, 25-26.

Hills, Rust. "Conversation: Arthur Miller and William Styron." *Audience* 1 (November/December 1971): 4-21.

Hughes, Catharine. "*The Crucible.*" *Plays, Politics, and Polemics.* New York: Drama Book Specialists, 1973: 15-25.

Hutchens, John K. "Mr. Miller Has a Change of Luck." *New York Times*, 23 February 1947, Sec. 2, pp. 1, 3.

Hyams, Barry. "A Theater; Heart and Mind." *Theater: The Annual of the Repertory Theater of lincoln Center* 1 (1964): 55-61.

James, Caryn. "On Film Credits List, That Miller is Arthur." *New York Times*, 22 November 1988, Sec. C, p. 17.

Johnson, Kirk. "Arthur Miller's Vision of Love Becomes a Movie." *New York Times*, 11 June 1989, Sec. H, pp. 19, 22-23.

Kaplan, James. "Miller's Crossing." *Vanity Fair* November 1991: 218-221, 241-248.

Kelly, Kevin. "Arthur Miller Emerges Again on Several Fronts." *Boston Globe*, 12 October 1980, pp. 81-82.

Lamos, Mark. "An Afternoon with Arthur Miller." *American Theatre* 3 (May 1986): 18-23.

Lardner, James. "Arthur Miller--Back in Control at 65." Washington Post, 26 October 1980, Sec. L, pp. 1, 5.

"Learning from a Performer: A Conversation with Arthur Miller." *Gamut* 1 (1982): 9-23.

Lenz, Harold. "At Sixes and Sevens--A Modern Theater Structure." Forum 11 (1973-1974): 73-79.

Mailer, Norman. "The Jewish Princess." *Marilyn.* New York: Grosset & Dunlap, 1973: 157-206.

Martin, Robert A. "Arthur Miller and the Meaning of Tragedy." *Modern Drama* 13 (May 1970): 34-39.

___. "Arthur Miller--Tragedy and Commitment." *Michigan Quarterly Review* 8 (Summer 1969): 176-178.

___. "The Creative Experience of Arthur Miller." *Educational Theatre Journal* 21 (October 1969): 310-317.

___. and Richard D. Meyer. "Arthur Miller on Plays and Playwriting." *Modern Drama* 19 (December 1976): 375-384.

Martine, James J. "'All in a Boiling Soup': An Interview with Arthur Miller." In *Critical Essays on Arthur Miller*. Ed. James J. Martine. Boston: G. K. Hall, 1979: 177-188.

Morley, Sheridan. "Miller on Miller." *Theatre World* 61 (March 1965): 4, 8.

Moss, Leonard. "'The Absence of the Tension': A Conversation with Arthur Miller." *Arthur Miller*. New York: Twayne, 1980: 107-122.

Parks, Michael. "*Salesman* Opens Door to Hearts of Peking Audience." *Los Angeles Times*, 8 May 1983, pp. 1, 18.

Rajakrishnan, V. "After Commitment: An Interview with Arthur Miller." *Theatre Journal* 32 (May 1980): 196-204.

Ratcliffe, Michael. "Miller's Russian Tale." *Observer*, 26 October 1986, p. 23.

Roudane, Matthew C. "An Interview with Arthur Miller." *Michigan Quarterly Review* 24 (1985): 373-389.

Sanoff, A. P. "The Theater Must Be Bread, Not Cake." *U.S. News & World Report* 11 January 1989: 54-55.

Schumach, Murray. "Arthur Miller Grew in Brooklyn." *New York Times*, 26 June 1975, p. 32.

___. "Miller Still a 'Salesman' for a Changing Theater." *New York Times*, 26 June 1975, p. 32.

Seligsohn, Leo. "Arthur Miller on the Eve of '*Creation*.'" *Newsday*, 26 November 1972, Sec. II, pp. 4-5, 28.

Shanley, John P. "Miller's '*Focus*' on TV Today." *New York Times*, 21 January 1962, Sec. II, p. 19.

Shenker, Israel. "Jewish Cultural Arts: The Big Debate." *New York Times*, 13 January 1976, p. 42.

Sylvester, Robert. "Brooklyn Boy Makes Good." *Saturday Evening Post* 16 July 1949: 26-27, 97-98, 100.

"Symposium: Playwrighting in America: Joyce Carol Oates, Arthur Miller, Eric Bentley." *Yale/Theater* 4 (1973): 8-27.

Terkel, Studs. "Studs Terkel Talks with Arthur Miller." *Saturday Review*, September 1980: 24-27.

Unger, Albert. "Arthur Miller Talks of His Holocaust Drama." *Christian Science Monitor*, 19 September 1980, p. 19.

Vajda, Miklos. "Playwrighting in America Today: A Telephone Interview with Arthur Miller." *New Hungarian Quarterly* 77 (1980): 123-124.

Wager, Walter. "Arthur Miller." In *The Playwrights Speak*. New York: Delta, 1967: 1-24.

Wain, John. "Arthur Miller." *Observer*, 8 September 1957, p. 5.

Weatherby, W. J. "Making *The Misfits*." *Manchester Guardian*, 3 November 1961, p. 8.

Wertham, Frederic. "Let the Salesman Beware." *New York Times Book Review*, 15 May 1949, pp. 4, 12.

Whitcomb, J. "Marilyn Monroe: The Sex Symbol versus the Good Wife." *Cosmopolitan*, December 1961: 53-57.

Wolf, Matt. "An Exile of Sorts Finds a Welcome." *New York Times*, 13 October 1991, Sec. H, p. 6.

Wolfert, Ira. "Arthur Miller, Playwright in Search of His Identity." *New York Herald-Tribune*, 25 January 1953, Sec. 4, p. 3.

Wren, Christopher S. "Willy Loman Gets China Territory." *New York Times*, 7 May 1983, p. 13.

Selected Periodical Publications (listed chronologically):

"Should Ezra Pound Be Shot?." *New Masses*, 25 December 1945, p. 6.

"The Plaster Masks." *Encore* 9 (April 1946): 424-432.

"Tragedy and the Common Man." *New York Times*, 27 February 1949, Sec. 2, pp. 1, 3.

"University of Michigan." *Holiday* 14 (December 1953): 68-71, 128-132, 136-137, 140-143.

"A Modest Proposal for Pacification of the Public Temper."
    Nation 3 July 1954: 5-8.
"A Boy Grew in Brooklyn." *Holiday* 17 (March 1955): 54-55,
    117, 119-120, 122-124.
"Picking a Cast." *New York Times*, 21 August 1955, Sec. 2, p. 1.
"The Family in Modern Drama." *Atlantic* 197 (April 1956): 35-
    41.
"The Playwright and the Atomic World." *Colorado Quarterly* 5
    (Autumn 1956): 117-137.
"The Writer in America." *Mainstream* 10 (July 1957): 43-46.
"Global Dramatist." *New York Times*, 21 July 1957, Sec. 2, p. 1.
"The Writer's Position in America." *Coastlines* 7 (Autumn
    1957): 38-40.
"The Shadows of the Gods: A Critical View of the American
    Theater." *Harper's* 217 (August 1958): 35-43.
"Bridge to a Savage World." *Esquire* 50 (October 1958): 185-
    190.
"My Wife Marilyn." *Life* 22 December 1958: 146-147.
"The Bored and the Violent." *Harper's* 225 (November 1962):
    50-52.
"A New Era in American Theater?." *Drama Survey* 3 (Spring
    1963): 70-71.
"Lincoln Repertory Theater--Challenge and Hope." *New York
    Times*, 19 January 1964, Sec. 2, pp. 1, 3.
"Foreword to *After the Fall*." *Saturday Evening Post* 1 February
    1964: 32.
"With Respect for Her Agony--But with Love." *Life* 7 February
    1964: 66.
"How the Nazi Trials Search the Hearts of All Germans."
    New York Herald-Tribune, 15 March 1964, p. 24.
"Our Guilt for the World's Evil." *New York Times Magazine*, 3
    January 1965, pp. 10-11, 48.
"The Writer as Independent Spirit: The Role of P.E.N." *Satur-
    day Review* 4 June 1966: 16-17.
"Arthur Miller: P.E.N., Politics and Literature." *Publisher's
    Weekly* 18 July 1966: 32-33.

"The Age of Abdication." *New York Times*, 23 December 1967, p. 40.

"On the Shooting of Robert Kennedy." *New York Times*, 8 June 1968, p. 30.

"Writers in Prison." *Encounter* 30 (June 1968): 60-61.

"The Battle of Chicago: From the Delegates' Side." *New York Times*, 15 September 1968, pp. 29-31, 122, 124, 126, 128.

"Are We Interested in Stopping the Killing?." *New York Times*, 8 June 1969, Sec. 2, p. 21.

"The War between Young and Old, or Why Willy Loman Can't Understand What's Happening." *McCall's* 97 (July 1970): 32.

"Banned in Russia." *New York Times*, 10 December 1970, p. 47.

"When Life Had at Least a Form." *New York Times*, 16 October 1971, p. 29.

"Politics as Theater." *New York Times*, 4 November 1972, p. 33.

"Miracles." *Esquire* 80 (September 1973): 112-115, 202-204.

"Sakharov, Detente and Liberty." *New York Times*, 5 July 1974, p. 21.

"What's Wrong with This Picture?." *Esquire* 82 (July 1974): 124-125, 170.

"The Limited Hang-Out: The Dialogues of Richard Nixon as a Drama of the Antihero." *Harper's* 249 (September 1974): 13-14, 16, 18-20.

"On True Identity." *New York Times Magazine*, 13 April 1975, p. 111.

"The Prague Winter." *New York Times*, 16 July 1975, p. 37.

"U.S. Urged to Guarantee Freedom of All Writers." *New York Times*, 19 November 1975, p. 25.

"Toward a New Foreign Policy." *Society* 13 (March-April 1976): 10, 15, 16.

"Our Most Widespread Dramatic Art Is Our Most Unfree." *New York Times*, 26 November 1978, Sec. 2, p. 33.

"Arthur Miller Stirs the Melting Pot That Didn't Melt." *U.S. News & World Report* 12 November 1979: 60-61.

"Clurmania: Address, May 6, 1979." *Nation* 26 May 1979: 606.

"In China." *Atlantic* 243 (March 1979): 90-103+.

"Saber and Me: Story of a Rare Friendship." *Vogue* 171 (November 1981): 211-212.

"The American Writer: The American Theater." *Michigan Quarterly Review* 21 (Winter 1982): 4-20.

"After the Spring." *House and Garden* 155 (April 1983): 104-105+.

"The Night Ed Murrow Struck Back." *Esquire* 100 (December 1983): 460-462+.

"Arthur Miller on McCarthy's Legacy: Address, April 30, 1984." *Harper's* 269 (July 1984): 11-12.

"The Face in the Mirror: Anti-Semitism Then and Now." *New York Times Book Review*, 14 October 1984, p. 3.

"Thoughts on a Burned House." *Architectural Digest* (November 1984): 44+.

"Dinner with the Ambassador." *Nation* 18 May 1985: 577+.

"A New Candor at Issyk-Kul." *Newsweek* 19 January 1987: 8.

"Okay, But Who Was I?." *Life* 10 (November 1987): 72-88.

"A Fabulous Appetite for Greatness." *New York Times Book Review*, 6 November 1988, pp. 12-13.

"Ibsen's Warning." *Index on Censorship* 18 (July-August 1989): 74-76.

"Death in Tiananmen." *New York Times*, 10 September 1989, Sec. 4, p. 31.

"Uneasy about the Germans." *New York Times Magazine*, 6 May 1990, pp. 46-47.

"In the Ayes of the Beholder: With Congress Debating Obscenity in Federally Funded Art, What Will Happen to Free Expression?" *Omni* 13 (February 1991): 10.

"The Measure of the Man." *Nation* 11 February 1991: 151-154.